CONTENTS

REPRISE: *Cinq portraits*

INTRODUCTION: What you will do and learn in *Reprise*

LESSON OPENERS

You will meet five young people from French-speaking areas: Éric (from France), Nadine (from Canada), Philippe (from Martinique), Vatea (from Tahiti), and Marie-France (from Switzerland). You will learn about their daily lives, their families, and their interests.

NOTES CULTURELLES

You will reacquaint yourself with France and the French-speaking world.

ACTIVITÉS

You will practice many of the communication skills
you learned last year, especially how

LA VIE DE TOUS LES JOURS

In these sections you will review how

STRUCTURE

You will review many important aspects of French grammar, especially: regular verbs in *-er*, *-ir*, and *-re*; the irregular verbs *être*, *avoir*, and *aller*; nouns and articles; forms and position of adjectives; subject and stress pronouns.

REPRISE CINQ PORTRAITS
Leçon 1 Éric

A1. EN VACANCES

It's the last week of vacation and the students below are still enjoying their free time. Write two sentences for each picture. First say *what* the people are doing. Then say that they are *not* studying. Follow the model.

▷ Marc *regarde la télé.*
Il n'étudie pas.

1. Nathalie _____

2. Nous _____

3. Tu _____

4. Jacqueline et Suzanne _____

5. Vous _____

6. Jacques et Monique _____

B1. POURQUOI?

Read what the following people do or do not do. Then say whether or not they like to do these things. Follow the models.

▷ **Henri danse avec Francine.** *Il aime danser avec Francine.*

▷ **Vous ne voyagez pas en bus.** *Vous n'aimez pas voyager en bus.*

1. Albert joue au tennis. _____

2. Nicole n'écoute pas la radio. _____

3. Je chante. _____

4. Tu ne téléphones pas à Marc. _____

5. Nous parlons français. _____

6. Vous n'étudiez pas. _____

7. Monsieur et Madame Moreau voyagent en train. _____

8. Charlotte ne parle pas anglais. _____

C1. AU TÉLÉPHONE

Imagine that you are at the home of Michèle, a French friend. She is on the phone with her cousin Jacqueline. Read how Michèle answers Jacqueline's questions. Then write the questions that Jacqueline asked to find out the information in italics. Use the appropriate interrogative expressions.

▷ Jacqueline: *À quelle heure est-ce que tu joues au tennis ?*
  Michèle: Je joue au tennis *à trois heures.*

1. Jacqueline: _____
   Michèle: Je joue *avec Marc.*

2. Jacqueline: _____
   Michèle: Il joue *assez bien.*

3. Jacqueline: _____
   Michèle: J'écoute *une cassette des Beatles.*

4. Jacqueline: _____
   Michèle: J'organise une boum *le 18 septembre.*

5. Jacqueline: _____
   Michèle: J'invite *Pierre et François.*

6. Jacqueline: _____
   Michèle: Ils habitent *à Toulouse.*

D1. OUI ET NON!

Read what the following people like to do or do not like to do. Tell them to act accordingly, using the appropriate *affirmative* or *negative* commands.

▷ **Jacques aime jouer au golf.**   *Joue au golf!*

▷ **Pauline déteste téléphoner.**   *Ne téléphone pas!*

1. Philippe aime chanter. _____

2. Roland et Antoine détestent danser. _____

3. Élisabeth et Sylvie aiment nager. _____

4. Charles déteste étudier. _____

5. Monsieur Richard aime voyager. _____

6. Madame Lamblet déteste voyager en train. _____

D2. SUGGESTIONS POUR LE WEEK-END

Imagine that you are spending Saturday afternoon with French friends. Suggest various activities that you all could do at the following times. Use the **nous** form of the imperative.

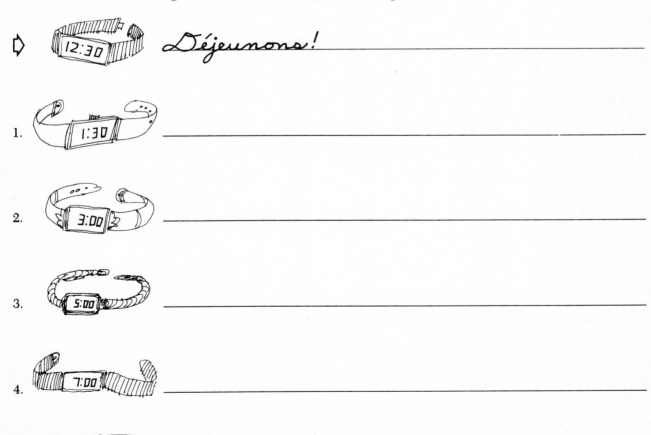

▷ 12:30   *Déjeunons!* _____

1. 1:30 _____

2. 3:00 _____

3. 5:00 _____

4. 7:00 _____

5. 8:00 _____

TRADUCTION

Give the French equivalent of each of the following sentences.

1. *Where do you live?*

   _____

2. *Do you travel often?*

   _____

3. *Does Jacques speak Spanish?*

   _____

4. *Yes, he speaks Spanish, but he prefers to speak French.*

   _____

5. *I want to study French because I would like to work in Paris.*

   _____

   _____

LA VIE DE TOUS LES JOURS   L'heure

Answer the following questions, giving the time to the nearest quarter hour.

1. Quelle heure est-il?

   _____

2. Généralement, à quelle heure est-ce que vous dînez?

   _____

3. À quelle heure est-ce que vous déjeunez?

   _____

4. À quelle heure est-ce que vous regardez la télé?

   _____

POUR COMMUNIQUER   Les choses que j'aime et les choses que je n'aime pas

State three things you like to do, and say how well you do them. Also state three things you do not like to do.

_____

_____

_____

_____

_____

_____

REPRISE   CINQ PORTRAITS
Leçon 2   Nadine

A1.   OUI OU NON?

Describe the following people. First say what they have, by filling in the first blank with the appropriate form of **avoir**. Then write a second sentence, using the appropriate affirmative or negative form of **être** and the word in parentheses.

▷   Michèle ___*a*___ un passeport français. *Elle n'est pas américaine.* (américaine?)

1.   Les voisins _____ une Mercédès. _____ (riches?)

2.   Vous _____ des idées stupides. _____ (intelligents?)

3.   Paul _____ un rendez-vous (*date*) avec Anne. _____ (triste?)

4.   Tu _____ un professeur très strict. _____ (content?)

5.   Nous _____ des amis sympathiques. _____ (contents?)

6.   J'_____ des idées intéressantes. _____ (pénible?)

B1.   EXPRESSION PERSONNELLE

Complete each of the sentences below with the names of at least *two* objects. Be sure to use the appropriate *indefinite article*.

1.   J'ai _____ .

2.   Mon meilleur ami a _____ .

3.   Les voisins ont _____ .

4.   Dans le garage, il y a _____ .

5.   Dans la classe (*classroom*), il y a _____ .

6.   Pour mon anniversaire (*birthday*), je voudrais avoir _____

B2.   TANT PIS! (*Too bad!*)

The following people are not doing certain things because they do not have the necessary items. Say which object they do not have.

▷   **Paul ne voyage pas.**   *Il n'a pas d'automobile.*
   (Il n'a pas de moto.)

1.   Irène ne joue pas au tennis. _____

2.   Je n'écoute pas mes disques. _____

3.   Vous n'écoutez pas le match de football. _____

4.   Tu n'étudies pas. _____

5.   Nous ne prenons (*take*) pas de photos. _____

B3. UN JEU DE CORRESPONDANCES

Match the nouns on the left with the nouns in the box on the right, according to the model.
(*Feminine* nouns are followed by an asterisk: *.)

▷   **aluminium**   *L'aluminium est un métal.*

1.	éléphant	_____	sport
2.	anglais	_____	art
3.	banane*	_____	fruit
4.	basketball	_____	science*
5.	guitare*	_____	métal
6.	musique*	_____	langue* (*language*)
7.	biologie*	_____	animal
			instrument de musique

B4.C1.   DESCRIPTIONS

Look carefully at the pictures below. Describe the people, using appropriate adjectives. Then describe
what these people own, using descriptive adjectives, if possible.

▷   **Caroline** *est blonde et petite. Elle a un grand chien.*

1.   **Jacques et Albert** _____

_____

2.   **Madame Dupont** _____

_____

3.   **Christine** _____

_____

4.   **Les voisins** _____

_____

C2. LE CONGRÈS INTERNATIONAL

The following young people are delegates at a world youth convention. Their cities of origin are given in parentheses. Give their nationalities. (Be sure to use the appropriate forms of the adjectives of nationality.)

⟹   (Chicago)   Linda   *est américaine* _____ .

1. (Berlin)   Karen et Ursula _____ .
2. (Avignon)   Paul et Jacques _____ .
3. (Mexico, D.F.)   Luisa _____ .
4. (Tokyo)   Tatsuo et Michio _____ .
5. (Québec)   Jacqueline et Monique _____ .
6. (Rome)   Silvia _____ .
7. (Londres)   Janet et Lynne _____ .
8. (San Francisco)   Tom et Jim _____ .
9. (Paris)   Suzanne et Nathalie _____ .
10. (Montréal)   Robert _____ .

C3. AU SALON DE L'AUTO (At the auto show)

The following cars are exhibited at the automobile show. Give your opinion of each car, using the feminine form of the adjective in parentheses. Be sure to put the adjective in its proper position.

⟹   (joli?)   **La Cadillac** *(n') est (pas) une jolie voiture* _____ .

⟹   (formidable?)   **La Jaguar** *(n') est (pas) une voiture formidable* _____ .

1. (petit?)   La Toyota _____ .
2. (économique?)   La Rolls Royce _____ .
3. (confortable?)   La Volvo _____ .
4. (grand?)   La Volkswagen _____ .
5. (bon?)   La Mercédès _____ .
6. (mauvais?)   La Pinto _____ .
7. (beau?)   L'Alfa Romeo _____ .
8. (pratique?)   La Lincoln Continental _____ .

D1. JACQUELINE

Jacqueline is talking about people she knows and things she has. Complete her descriptions with **C'est** or **Il est/Elle est,** as appropriate.

1. J'ai un petit ami. _____ espagnol. _____ un garçon sympathique.
2. J'ai une amie. _____ une fille très intéressante. _____ très drôle aussi.
3. J'ai une voiture. _____ une Toyota. _____ une voiture japonaise.
4. J'ai un téléviseur. _____ français. _____ très bon.

TRADUCTION

Give the French equivalent of each of the following sentences.

1. *I have a dog but I don't have a cat.*

   _____

2. *Paul has a Spanish guitar and French records.*

   _____

3. *Mélanie and Nicole have a German car, but they are not German.*

   _____

   _____

4. *Look at the girl. It's Catherine. She is a friend. She is very nice.*

   _____

   _____

5. *We have a dog. He is small, but he is a very intelligent dog.*

   _____

   _____

LA VIE DE TOUS LES JOURS   Un peu de maths

Complete each of the following equations by writing out the missing number.

a. dix + cinq = _____

b. dix + huit = _____

c. dix + onze = _____

d. trente + douze = _____

e. quarante-huit + quatre = _____

f. vingt-cinq × deux = _____

POUR COMMUNIQUER   Auto-portrait (*Self-portrait*)

Describe yourself. (What is your nationality? the color of your hair? your size? Are you a good student?)
Then describe three or four objects you own.

_____

_____

_____

_____

_____

_____

REPRISE CINQ PORTRAITS
Leçon 3 Philippe

A1. PERDUS (*Lost*)

Help the following people find their way. To do this, match each person with the appropriate destination in the box on the right.

▷ **Le mécanicien** *va à la station-service* .

1. Le chimiste _____ .	le théâtre
2. Le professeur _____ .	la station-service
3. L'athlète _____ .	l'ambassade (*embassy*)
4. L'acteur _____ .	le stade
5. L'ambassadeur _____ .	l'école
6. Le pilote _____ .	le laboratoire
7. Le touriste _____ .	le musée
	l'aéroport

A2. QU'EST-CE QU'ILS FONT? (*What are they doing?*)

Describe what the following people are doing. Use the suggested words and write complete sentences. Be sure to give the right forms of the verbs. Make the contractions with **à** and **de** when necessary.

▷ **Béatrice / téléphoner à / le garçon anglais**
Béatrice téléphone au garçon anglais.

1. le professeur / parler à / l'élève canadien

_____

2. le guide / parler à / les touristes

_____

3. nous / jouer à / le football

_____

4. Thérèse / jouer de / le piano

_____

5. vous / arriver de / la poste

_____

6. nous / rentrer de / l'école

_____

7. tu / parler de / les amis de Bernard

_____

8. je / téléphoner à / les cousins de Colette

_____

B1. OÙ ET POURQUOI?

For the people listed below, assign a destination (column A). Then say what they are going to do there, using an activity from column B. Be logical! (If you do not remember the gender of the nouns in column A, look at the **Vocabulaire pratique** on page 28 of your textbook.)

A	B
cinéma	changer des dollars
restaurant	nager
stade	étudier
plage	regarder les oiseaux
banque	regarder les sculptures
bibliothèque	regarder un western
musée	jouer au football
campagne	dîner

▷ Tu *vas au musée. Tu vas regarder les sculptures.*

1. Jacques _____

2. Nous _____

3. Vous _____

4. Monsieur et Madame Martin _____

5. Les élèves _____

6. Je _____

7. Tu _____

B2. WEEK-END

Say that this weekend the people below are *not* going to do what they are doing now.

aujourd'hui: **ce week-end:**

▷ **Paul étudie.**   *Il ne va pas étudier.* _____

1. Les voisins travaillent.   _____

2. Monsieur Bernard voyage.   _____

3. Nous déjeunons à la cafétéria.   _____

4. J'étudie à la bibliothèque.   _____

5. Tu écoutes le professeur.   _____

6. Vous allez au lycée.   _____

C1. UN PEU DE GÉOGRAPHIE

Arrange the countries below according to the continent on which they are located. Be sure to use the correct article with each country.

Égypte, Danemark, Chili,

Japon, Nigeria, Tunisie,

Chine, Portugal, Canada,

Argentine, Luxembourg,

Allemagne, Sénégal,

États-Unis

Europe	Amérique	Asie	Afrique
			l'Égypte

C2. OÙ?

The following people are in their country of origin. Say what they are doing, using the verb in parentheses. Be sure to use the appropriate preposition to introduce the name of the country.

▷ **Luisa est espagnole. (étudier)**   *Elle étudie en Espagne.* _____

1. François est français. (habiter)   _____
2. Vous êtes canadiens. (travailler)   _____
3. Nous sommes américains. (étudier)   _____
4. Janet est anglaise. (voyager)   _____
5. Tu es italien. (habiter)   _____

TRADUCTION

Give the French equivalent of each of the following sentences.

1. *I go to school by bus.*

   _____

2. *Pierre goes to the stadium on foot.*

   _____

3. *Are you going to work tomorrow?*

   _____

4. *Hélène is going to the beach, but she is not going to swim.*

   _____

LA VIE DE TOUS LES JOURS   Activités

Plan four activities for the coming week. Say on which day and what time of day you are going to do them.

▷ *Jeudi soir je vais aller au cinéma.* _____

1. _____
2. _____
3. _____
4. _____

POUR COMMUNIQUER   Les vacances

In a short paragraph, describe your summer vacation. Where do you usually go? What are you going to do next summer? What are you not going to do?

En général _____

_____

_____

_____

Les vacances prochaines (*Next vacation*) _____

_____

_____

_____

REPRISE CINQ PORTRAITS
Leçon 4 Vatea

A1. ANONYMAT (*Anonymity*)

Imagine that you do not want to reveal the names of the people below. Rewrite the sentences, using only *subject* and *stress pronouns*.

▷ **Hélène et Anne dînent avec Louis et Marc.** *Elles dînent avec eux.*

1. Henri travaille pour Monsieur Durand. _____

2. Jacqueline voyage avec ses amis américains. _____

3. Sylvie et Stéphanie sont avec Thomas. _____

4. Albert dîne avec Nicole. _____

5. Jean et Paul dansent avec Anne et Lise. _____

B1. IL PLEUT (*It's raining*)

Because of a rainstorm, everyone is staying home. Say what the following people are doing. In each sentence use the appropriate form of the verb in parentheses and the construction **chez** + *stress pronoun*.

▷ (déjeuner) **Madame Martin** *déjeune chez elle* _____.

1. (étudier) J'_____.

2. (travailler) Monsieur Pascal _____.

3. (regarder la télé) Bernard et Henri _____.

4. (dîner) Monique et Nicole _____.

5. (travailler) Tu _____.

C1. EMPRUNTS (*Borrowed items*)

Whenever Pierre borrows something, he tags it with the name of its owner. Identify each of the objects below, according to the model.

▷ *C'est la guitare de René.*

1. _____

2. _____

3. _____

4. _____

5. _____

D1. WEEK-END

Describe the weekend activities of the people below. Select an activity from column A and two people from column B. Use the appropriate *possessive adjectives*.

A		B		
déjeuner	visiter un musée	(le) frère	(l')ami Thomas	(les) parents
aller au cinéma	aller à la campagne	(la) sœur	(l')amie Catherine	(les) amis
jouer au tennis			(les) voisins	(les) cousins

⇨ Henri *visite un musée avec son frère et ses cousins* .

1. Tu _____ .

2. Je _____ .

3. Sylvie _____ .

4. Vous _____ .

5. Bernard et Paul _____ .

6. Nous _____ .

7. Hélène et Marie _____ .

TRADUCTION

Give the French equivalent of each of the following sentences.

1. *I am not home. I am at Paul's house.* _____

2. *François is going to the neighbors'.* _____

3. *Charles has Nicole's guitar.* _____

4. *My cousin Marc is inviting his friend Christine.* _____

LA VIE DE TOUS LES JOURS   Joyeux anniversaire! (*Happy birthday!*)

Complete the sentences below with the appropriate birthday dates.

1. Mon anniversaire est _____ .

2. L'anniversaire de mon père est _____ .

3. L'anniversaire de ma mère est _____ .

4. L'anniversaire de mon meilleur ami est _____ .

POUR COMMUNIQUER   Votre meilleur(e) ami(e)

Describe your best friend in three sentences. Then describe three members of his or her family.

_____

_____

_____

_____

REPRISE   CINQ PORTRAITS
Leçon 5   Marie-France

V1.   LE MAGAZINE DE MODE (*The fashion magazine*)

Imagine that you are working for a fashion magazine. Describe the four models below by saying which clothes and accessories they are wearing. Give a color for each item of clothing.

| **Marie-Laure** | **Jean-Édouard** | **André** | **Isabelle** |

1.   Marie-Laure porte _____
     _____ .

2.   Jean-Édouard porte _____
     _____ .

3.   André porte _____
     _____ .

4.   Isabelle porte _____
     _____ .

A1.   AU GRAND MAGASIN (*At the department store*)

Henri and Jacqueline are shopping. Henri wants to know which items Jacqueline is interested in.
Complete the dialogs, according to the model.

Henri:

➪ *Quel* disque est-ce que tu écoutes?

1.   _____ chaussures est-ce que tu choisis?

2.   _____ veste est-ce que tu aimes?

3.   _____ livres est-ce que tu regardes?

4.   _____ appareil-photo est-ce que tu préfères?

5.   _____ vélo est-ce que tu as?

Jacqueline:

J'écoute ce disque-ci.

_____

_____

_____

_____

B1.C1. OUI OU NON?

Read about the following people. Then describe what they do or do not do. Complete each of the sentences below with the appropriate *affirmative* or *negative* form of the verb in parentheses.

⇨ **Jacques est impatient.** *Il n'attend pas* ses amis. (attendre)

1. Ces garçons sont timides. _____ souvent. (rougir)

2. Nous sommes dans un magasin. _____ des vêtements. (choisir)

3. Tu n'étudies pas. _____ à tes examens. (réussir)

4. M. Bernard aime déjeuner au restaurant. _____ (maigrir)

5. Alice et Louise sont des filles modèles. _____ à leurs parents. (obéir)

6. Vous mangez (*eat*) beaucoup. _____ (grossir)

7. Nous sommes à l'aéroport. _____ des avions. (entendre)

8. Luc travaille dans une pharmacie. _____ de l'aspirine. (vendre)

9. Aujourd'hui je suis chez moi. _____ à mes amis. (rendre visite)

10. Vous n'étudiez pas. _____ votre temps. (perdre)

11. Tu es un mauvais élève. _____ aux questions (répondre) du professeur.

12. Isabelle joue très bien au tennis. _____ souvent. (perdre)

D1. POURQUOI?

Read what the following students do, and ask the reason why. In each of your questions use a subject pronoun (**il/elle/ils/elles**) and *inversion*.

⇨ **Paul étudie l'anglais.** *Pourquoi étudie-t-il l'anglais ?*

1. Hélène étudie l'espagnol. _____

2. Robert invite cette fille. _____

3. Les voisins voyagent souvent. _____

4. Pauline et Louise travaillent. _____

5. Albert va à Paris. _____

6. Sylvie et Nicole vont au Canada. _____

7. Isabelle rougit. _____

8. Marc vend sa guitare. _____

9. Henri est à l'hôpital. _____

10. Ces filles sont au stade. _____

D2. CURIOSITÉ

Whenever Jean-Pierre makes a statement about his vacation plans, he asks Martine to give him similar information. Write out each of Jean-Pierre's questions, using inversion and the appropriate interrogative expression. (The words in italics indicate the information he is looking for. If necessary, you may want to review the interrogative expressions on page 10 of your textbook.)

▷ **Je vais *en Italie*. Et toi,** _où vas-tu_____ ?

1. Je voyage *en autobus*. Et toi, _____ ?

2. Je voyage *avec des amis*. Et toi, _____ ?

3. Je voyage *parce que j'aime voyager*. Et toi, _____ ?

4. Je rends visite *à mon cousin*. Et toi, _____ ?

5. Je rentre *en octobre*. Et toi, _____ ?

6. Je rentre *en avion*. Et toi, _____ ?

TRADUCTION

Give the French equivalent of each of the following sentences. Use inversion for the questions in items 1, 3, and 4.

1. *Which hat are you choosing?*

    _____

2. *I like these shoes over here, but I do not like those sandals over there.*

    _____

    _____

3. *I am going to visit Pierre. Where does he live?*

    _____

    _____

4. *You play tennis with Caroline. How does she play?*

    _____

    _____

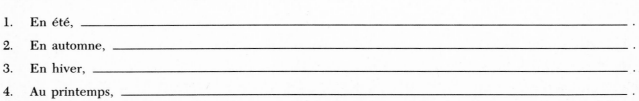

LA VIE DE TOUS LES JOURS   Les quatre saisons

Describe the weather in your region for each season.

1. En été, _____ .

2. En automne, _____ .

3. En hiver, _____ .

4. Au printemps, _____ .

POUR COMMUNIQUER   Vos vêtements

Describe the clothes and accessories you are wearing now. Give their colors.

Je porte _____

_____

_____

_____

_____

_____

_____

Récréation culturelle

Le passeport de Jean-François

Quand on voyage, on a besoin d'un (*you need a*) passeport. Regardez le passeport suivant (*following*) et répondez aux questions.

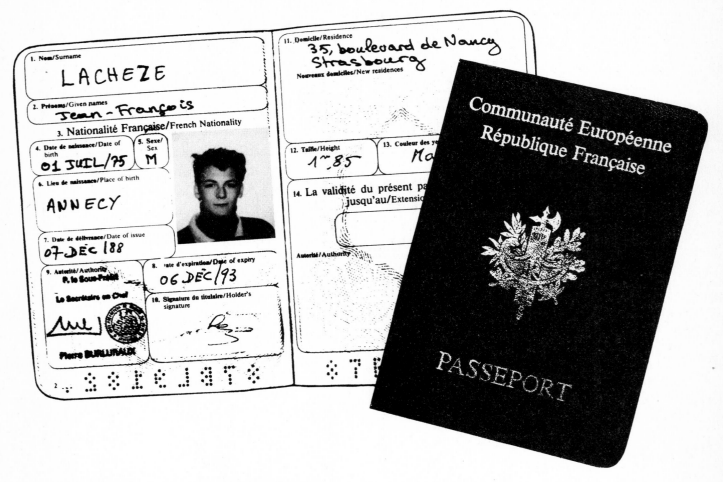

1. Quel est le nom (*name*) de la personne?

   _____

2. Quelle est sa nationalité?

   _____

3. Quelle est sa date de naissance (*birth*)?

   _____

4. Quel âge a-t-il maintenant?

   _____

Reprise

Récréation culturelle

Bon voyage!

Imaginez que vous avez un cousin à Paris. Il vous invite à passer les vacances chez lui. Avant votre départ (*departure*), vous lui envoyez (*send him*) un télégramme où vous annoncez l'heure de votre arrivée.

N° 698 TÉLÉGRAMME

Services spéciaux demandés : (voir au verso)	Inscrire en **CAPITALES** l'adresse complète (rue, n° bloc, bâtiment, escalier, etc...), le texte et la signature (une lettre par case ; **laisser une case blanche entre les mots**).

Pour accélérer la remise des télégrammes indiquer le numéro de téléphone (1) ou de télex (3) du destinataire
TF_____TLX_____   Nom et adresse

TEXTE et éventuellement signature très lisible

ARRIVE ROISSY MARDI 18 JUILLET
13h40 VOL AIR FRANCE 242
AMITIES
                PATRICK

(Roissy est le nom du principal aéroport international de Paris.)

GLOSSAIRE: **vol** *flight*   **amitiés** *all the best*

Maintenant vous êtes dans l'avion qui va à Paris. Avant l'arrivée, l'hôtesse vous donne (*gives you*) une carte de débarquement. Remplissez (*Fill out*) cette carte en français.

CARTE DE DÉBARQUEMENT
DISEMBARKATION CARD

1 **NOM** : _____
NAME (en caractère d'imprimerie — please print)

Nom de jeune fille : _____
Maiden name

Prénoms : _____
Given names

2 **Date de naissance** : _____
Date of birth   (jour, mois, année — day, month, year)

3 **Lieu de naissance** : _____
Place of birth

4 **Nationalité** : _____
Nationality

5 **Profession** : _____
Occupation

6 **Domicile** : _____
Permanent address

_____

7 **Aéroport de débarquement** : _____
Airport of disembarkation

Récréation culturelle

Voyageons en train!

En France, le train est un mode (*means*) de transport très populaire. Les trains français sont en effet (*in fact*) rapides, confortables et bon marché. Ils ont aussi l'avantage d'être toujours à l'heure (*on time*). Les chemins de fer (*railroads*) français dépendent d'une (*belong to a*) grande compagnie nationale, la SNCF (Société Nationale des Chemins de fer Français).

Dans cette publicité (*advertisement*), la SNCF propose certains (*some*) voyages dans des pays voisins (*neighboring*) de la France.

avec le train,
porte ouverte sur
L'EUROPE

Week-ends, séjours, minicroisières
TOURISME SNCF
✈ **voyages**

week-ends au départ de paris

voyage	date de départ	*jours de voyage	
allemagne			
munich	chaque vendredi du 3 janvier au 30 mai et du 19 octobre au 26 décembre	4	750 F
angleterre			
londres	tous les jours du 28 mars au 24 octobre	4	875 F
belgique			
bruges	7 juin - 5 juillet - 2 août - 6 septembre - 9 novembre	2	630 F
bruxelles - bruges - anvers	29 mars - 17 mai - 12 juillet	3	1.040 F
espagne			
le pays basque espagnol	28 mars - 16 mai	5	1.135 F
costa brava - barcelone	28 mars - 16 mai - 11 juillet - 14 août	5	1.260 F
madrid	chaque jeudi du 2 janvier au 19 juin et du 4 septembre au 20 novembre	5	1.350 F
madrid - tolède	16 mai - 14 août - 8 novembre	5	1.650 F
italie			
milan et les lacs	5 septembre	4	1.035 F
florence	chaque jour du 2 janvier au 30 octobre	5	1.390 F
luxembourg			
luxembourg	24 mai - 21 juin - 23 août - 27 septembre	2	680 F
suisse			
berne	chaque vendredi du 3 janvier au 31 octobre	4	590 F
l'oberland bernois	9 mai - 19 septembre	4	1.050 F
lucerne et le mont rigi	13 juin - 12 septembre	4	1.150 F

1. Mettez le nom de ces pays sur la carte (*map*).

Choisissez l'un de ces voyages.

2. Quel pays allez-vous visiter?

_____

3. Combien de jours allez-vous rester dans ce pays?

_____

4. Quel est le prix du voyage?

_____

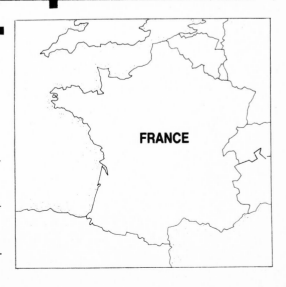

FRANCE

Récréation culturelle

Un week-end à Genève

Imaginez que vous habitez à Paris. Vous décidez de passer le week-end à Genève. Vous voulez prendre le TGV (train à grande vitesse [*speed*]). Les TGV sont des trains très rapides (*fast*). Ils vont à une vitesse de 270 kilomètres à l'heure. Ces trains relient (*link*) Paris aux grandes villes de l'Est et du Sud de la France. Ils relient aussi Paris avec certaines grandes villes européennes, comme (*such as*) Genève.

Étudiez attentivement (*carefully*) l'horaire (*schedule*).

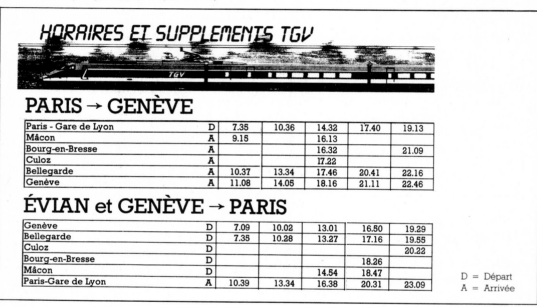

HORAIRES ET SUPPLEMENTS TGV

PARIS → GENÈVE

Paris - Gare de Lyon	D	7.35	10.36	14.32	17.40	19.13
Mâcon	A	9.15		16.13		
Bourg-en-Bresse	A			16.32		21.09
Culoz	A			17.22		
Bellegarde	A	10.37	13.34	17.46	20.41	22.16
Genève	A	11.08	14.05	18.16	21.11	22.46

ÉVIAN et GENÈVE → PARIS

Genève	D	7.09	10.02	13.01	16.50	19.29
Bellegarde	D	7.35	10.28	13.27	17.16	19.55
Culoz	D					20.22
Bourg-en-Bresse	D				18.26	
Mâcon	D			14.54	18.47	
Paris-Gare de Lyon	A	10.39	13.34	16.38	20.31	23.09

D = Départ
A = Arrivée

1. Mettez le nom des quatre villes principales—Paris, Mâcon, Bourg-en-Bresse, Genève—sur la carte.

2. Vous désirez arriver à Genève pour le dîner. À quelle heure allez-vous partir de Paris?

_____

3. Dans quelle gare prenez-vous le TGV?

_____

4. Quelle est la durée (*duration*) du voyage?

_____

5. Dimanche, vous allez rentrer avec le train de 19.29. Combien d'arrêts (*stops*) est-ce qu'il y a entre Genève et Paris?

Récréation culturelle

Quand vous voyagez avec le TGV, vous avez besoin non seulement (*not only*) d'un billet (*ticket*) de train, mais aussi d'une réservation. Voici votre réservation.

1.   Combien coûte la réservation? _____

2.   Quel est le numéro de votre voiture? _____

3.   Est-ce que vous voyagez en première classe ou en deuxième classe? _____

Maintenant, votre week-end à Genève est fini. Envoyez un télégramme à votre famille à Paris. Dans ce télégramme, indiquez à quelle gare et à quelle heure vous allez arriver à Paris. (Comme modèle, utilisez (*use*) le télégramme de la page 20.)

N° 698   TÉLÉGRAMME

Services spéciaux demandés : (voir au verso)	Inscrire en **CAPITALES** l'adresse complète (rue, n° bloc, bâtiment, escalier, etc...), le texte et la signature (une lettre par case ; **laisser une case blanche entre les mots**).		
	Pour accélérer la remise des télégrammes indiquer le numéro de téléphone (1) ou de télex (3) du destinataire TF_____TLX_____	Nom et adresse	

TEXTE et éventuellement signature très lisible

Récréation culturelle

Bonjour, le monde francophone!

Une compagnie de bonne compagnie.

AIR CANADA

royal air maroc
Une compagnie 4 continents.

SABENA
BELGIAN *World* AIRLINES
AMERIQUE · AFRIQUE · EUROPE · MOYEN ORIENT

AIR FRANCE ////
Le meilleur de la France vers le monde.

swissair ✚

AIR AFRIQUE
une grande compagnie dans un grand continent

Un certain nombre de pays (ou groupes de pays) ont leur compagnie aérienne (*airline*) nationale (ou multinationale). Les compagnies aériennes ci-dessus (*above*) desservent (*fly to*) des villes où l'on parle français.

Imaginez que vous désirez visiter les villes suivantes. Pour chaque (*each*) ville, dites dans quel pays elle est située (*located*) et quelle compagnie aérienne vous allez prendre.

VILLES	PAYS	COMPAGNIES AÉRIENNES
Montréal		
Marseille		
Bruxelles		
Genève		
Dakar		
Casablanca		
Lausanne		
Abidjan		

Récréation culturelle

Un voyage au Canada

Regardez cette brochure.

AIR FRANCE *Vacances*

3 650 F vol seul aller et retour

MONTRÉAL

AVION-HOTEL-AUTO

■ AVION

Vols et tarifs Air France
aller et retour.
MONTRÉAL au départ de :

PARIS	3 650 F

Liaisons aéroport/ville : 53 km.
En car : 45 mn. Prix 9 dollars.

■ HÔTEL

Prix par personne et par nuit avec
petit déjeuner continental au Baccarat
et en hébergement seul au Méridien.

Hôtel Le Baccarat
■□□□□ catégorie touriste

475 Ouest Sherbrooke - Montréal.
Tél. : (1) (514) 842.39.61.
Votre chambre avec salle de bains, air
conditionné, télévision, téléphone, réfrigérateur, kitchenette.

Exemples de prix

chambre triple	160 F
chambre double	230 F
chambre individuelle	365 F

Hôtel Méridien
■■■■■ catégorie luxe

4 complexe Desjardins - Montréal.
Tél. : (1) (514) 285.14.50.

Votre chambre : salle de bains, air
conditionné, radio, télévision couleur.

Exemples de prix

chambre double	370 F
chambre individuelle	590 F

■ AUTO

Prix par voiture en kilométrage illimi-
té, assurance au tiers et taxes locales
incluses. Location minimum : 5 jours.
Cat. A : Ford Escort.
Cat. C : Ford Tempo.

EXEMPLES DE PRIX

5 jours HERTZ, cat. A......	992 F
7 jours HERTZ, cat. C......	1 374 F

HERTZ : Aéroport - Tél. : 476.33.85.
Ville : Hertz at the Bay - 1475 Aylmer
Street/de Maisonneuve Blrd
Tél. : 842.85.37.

BON A SAVOIR

- **Formalités** : passeport.
- **Monnaie** : 1 dollar canadien
  = 4,33 F environ

GLOSSAIRE: **vol seul** flight only **aller et retour** *round trip*

1. Quelle compagnie aérienne a publié (*published*) cette brochure? _____

2. Quel voyage propose-t-elle? _____

3. Combien coûte l'avion? _____

4. Vous avez le choix (*choice*) entre deux hôtels. Comment s'appellent-ils? _____

   _____

   Lequel (*Which*) est le plus cher? _____

5. Combien coûte une Ford Escort pour 5 jours? _____

UNITÉ 1: *C'est la vie!*

INTRODUCTION: What you will do and learn in *Unité 1*

LESSON OPENERS

You will read about Jean-Louis and Béatrice, who are organizing a party. You will be asked to answer five easy questions about French culture and geography. And you will be challenged to solve a bank burglary that took place during a power failure.

NOTES CULTURELLES

You will learn about certain aspects of a young French person's life (parties, driver's license) and of French life in general (telephones, outdoor markets, the family car). And you will learn more about the French-speaking world (Corsica, Guadeloupe, Marseille).

ACTIVITÉS

You will continue to practice many of the communication
skills you learned last year, especially how   *pages in your textbook*

to talk about a certain quantity or amount of something	62
to describe your leisure-time activities	64–65
to talk about your money	76
to describe or ask questions about past events	78–79, 80–81, 84, 86–87, 94–95
to express what you have just done	92

STRUCTURE

You will continue to review some important aspects of French grammar, especially the partitive article, the pronoun *on*, and the *passé composé*. You will also review many irregular French verbs, including *prendre, boire, faire, vouloir, mettre, sortir,* and *venir*. In addition you will learn two *new* structures: the verb *conduire* (to drive) and the expression *il faut* (it is necessary).

UNITÉ 1   C'EST LA VIE!

Leçon 1   Une allergie

V1.   «CHEZ JACQUELINE»

Imagine that you are working in a French restaurant called **«CHEZ JACQUELINE»**. You are preparing the menu of the day. For each category, give at least *two* choices.

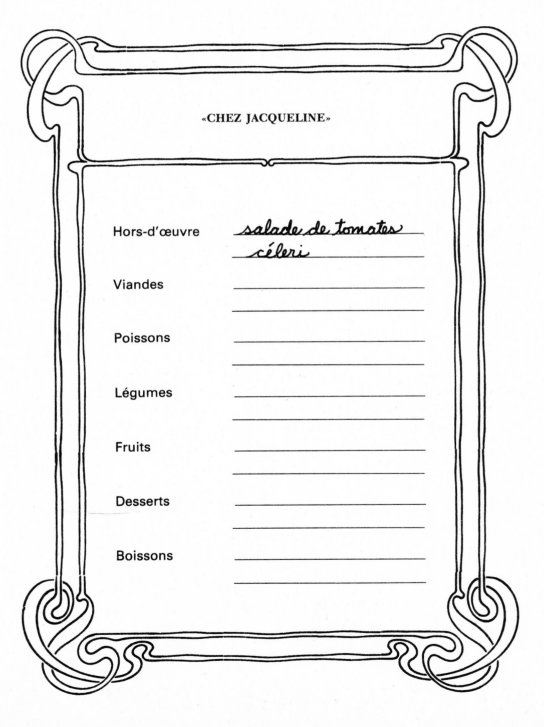

«CHEZ JACQUELINE»

Hors-d'œuvre   *salade de tomates*
              céleri

Viandes   _____

Poissons   _____

Légumes   _____

Fruits   _____

Desserts   _____

Boissons   _____

A1. L'INSTITUT DE LANGUES

The students below are preparing for their summer vacations by learning the language spoken in the city they are going to visit. Write sentences saying which of the following languages they are learning: **l'espagnol / l'anglais / l'allemand.** Use the appropriate forms of the verb **apprendre.**

▷ Olivier va à Barcelone.   *Il apprend l'espagnol.*

1. Jacques va à Mexico. _____

2. Ses sœurs vont à Chicago. _____

3. Nous allons à Berlin. _____

4. Tu vas à Buenos Aires. _____

5. Vous allez à Munich. _____

6. Thérèse va à Londres. _____

7. Je vais à Hambourg. _____

8. Henri et François vont à Vancouver. _____

B1. LE RÉGIME DE NICOLE (*Nicole's diet*)

Nicole is on a special diet where she can have everything *except* dairy products. Say whether or not the following items are permitted. Make *affirmative* or *negative* sentences, using the verbs in parentheses and the appropriate *partitive articles*.

▷ la limonade?   *Oui, elle boit de la limonade.*   (boire)

1. le jambon? _____ (manger)

2. le beurre? _____ (prendre)

3. la salade? _____ (manger)

4. la glace? _____ (commander)

5. les spaghetti? _____ (prendre)

6. le yaourt? _____ (acheter)

7. le sucre? _____ (prendre)

8. l'eau minérale? _____ (boire)

B2. **LES INGRÉDIENTS NÉCESSAIRES**

The following people are preparing various dishes for a dinner party. Complete the sentences with the necessary ingredients.

1. Monique fait un «banana split» avec *des bananes et* _____

   _____ .

2. Paul fait une omelette au jambon avec _____

   _____ .

3. Jacques fait une salade de tomates avec _____

   _____ .

4. Nicole fait une salade de fruits avec _____

   _____ .

5. Isabelle fait une «Quiche Lorraine» avec _____

   _____ .

6. Bernard fait des sandwichs au poulet avec _____

   _____ .

B3.C1. **À TABLE**

Complete each of the sentences below with the appropriate form of **boire** and a beverage of your choice.

1. Au petit déjeuner, je _____ .

2. À la cafétéria de l'école, nous _____ .

3. Au dîner, mon père _____ .

4. Les jeunes Américains _____ .

5. Est-ce que vous _____ ?

6. Quand il fait chaud, est-ce que tu _____ ?

Unité un **29**

B4.D1. OUI OU NON?

Read about the following people, and say whether or not they engage in the activities indicated in parentheses. Make *affirmative* or *negative* statements, using the appropriate forms of **faire** and the activities in parentheses.

▷ **Henri grossit.** *Il ne fait pas de sport.*   (le sport?)

1. Valérie veut maigrir. _____ (le jogging?)

2. J'habite en Floride. _____ (le ski?)

3. Mes cousins habitent à Hawaii. _____ (la planche à voile?)

4. Vous aimez la nature. _____ (le camping?)

5. Tu n'aimes pas prendre de risques (*risks*). _____ (l'alpinisme?)

   _____

6. Nous n'aimons pas les sports violents. _____ (le hockey?)

   _____

7. François est canadien. _____ (le patin à glace?)

8. Vous êtes très grand. _____ (le basketball?)

TRADUCTION

Give the French equivalent of each of the following sentences.

1. *Are you having yogurt or ice cream?*

   _____

2. *I am ordering salad because I do not like meat.*

   _____

3. *Don't drink wine! Drink mineral water!*

   _____

4. *Paul is going shopping because he is going to do the cooking.*

   _____

   _____

POUR COMMUNIQUER   À la cafétéria de l'école

Describe a typical meal at your school cafeteria. Say which foods you like and which ones you do not like.

_____

_____

_____

_____

_____

UNITÉ 1   C'EST LA VIE!

Leçon 2   Petits problèmes simples

A1.   **AU VOLANT** (*At the wheel*)

The people below have cars made in the countries where they live. Say which of the following cars they drive. In your sentences, use the appropriate forms of **conduire.**

> **une Fiat / une Mercédès / une Chevrolet / une Jaguar / une Renault / une Toyota**

1.   Mon cousin est anglais. _____

2.   Nous sommes américains. _____

3.   Je suis français. _____

4.   Tu es japonais. _____

5.   Vous êtes italiens. _____

6.   Karen et Ursula sont allemandes. _____

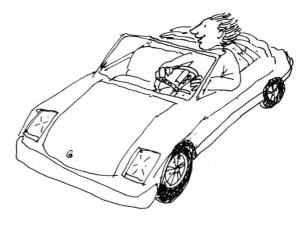

B1.   **EN ZUTOPIE**

Jacques read a short article about Zutopie, an imaginary island, and its inhabitants, the Zutopians. He prepared a report for school in which he began each sentence with **on.** Write out what he said.

L'ARTICLE: Les Zutopiens ne travaillent pas. Ils jouent de la guitare. Ils dansent dans les rues (*streets*). Ils aiment la musique. Ils portent des jolis costumes. Ils vont à la plage. Ils font du sport. Ils ne vont pas à l'école. Ils n'étudient pas. Ils sont toujours contents.

LE RAPPORT DE JACQUES: *En Zutopie, on ne travaille pas.*
On _____

_____

_____

_____

_____

B2. CONSÉQUENCES

Say whether or not people who do the first thing in parentheses usually do the second. Use the subject pronoun **on.**

▷ **(conduire bien / avoir des accidents?)**

Quand on conduit bien, on n'a pas d'accidents.

1. (étudier / apprendre?)

   _____

2. (faire du sport / grossir?)

   _____

3. (aller à la plage / porter un manteau?)

   _____

4. (organiser une boum / inviter des amis?)

   _____

5. (être sympathique / avoir beaucoup d'amis?)

   _____

C1. SHOPPING

Read how much money the people below have. Then say what they can buy with this money.

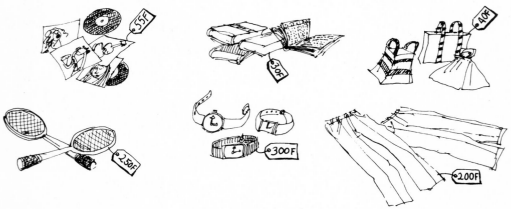

▷ Éric a 150 francs.   *Il peut acheter dix livres (un pantalon, trois disques...).*

1. Joséphine a 200 francs.   _____
2. Nous avons 250 francs.   _____
3. Vous avez 300 francs.   _____
4. Mes sœurs ont 400 francs.   _____
5. J'ai 450 francs.   _____
6. Tu as 500 francs.   _____

C2. QUAND ON VEUT . . .

Assign each of the people below an objective from column A. Then say where this person must go (column B) to achieve this objective. Use the appropriate forms of **vouloir** and **devoir,** according to the model. Be logical!

	A			**B**	
dîner	acheter de l'aspirine		à Québec	au restaurant	
nager	être médecin		à la campagne	à la piscine	
parler français	faire du camping		à la pharmacie	au stade	
faire du sport			à l'université		

▷ Nathalie *veut faire du sport. Elle doit aller au stade.*

1. Paul _____

2. Mes parents _____

3. Vous _____

4. Tu _____

5. Je _____

6. Nous _____

C3. BONS CONSEILS (*Good advice*)

Imagine that you write a newspaper column in which you give advice to your readers. Write out short answers to the following letters. Use the appropriate forms of **devoir / pouvoir / vouloir** . . . and your imagination.

▷ «**Je suis bon en maths. Quelle profession est-ce que je peux choisir?**»

Tu peux être programmeur. Tu peux aussi être architecte. Si tu es très bon en maths, tu peux être ingénieur.

1. «Je voudrais être médecin, mais je ne suis pas très bon en biologie. Qu'est-ce que je dois faire?»

_____

_____

2. «J'ai un ami français. Il veut passer trois mois dans une école américaine, mais il n'a pas beaucoup d'argent (*money*). Qu'est-ce qu'il peut faire?»

_____

_____

3. «Mes parents vont aller en France en décembre. Qu'est-ce qu'ils peuvent faire là-bas?»

_____

_____

4. «Nous voulons faire une surprise à notre professeur pour son anniversaire (*birthday*). Qu'est-ce que nous pouvons faire?»

_____

_____

D1. QU'EST-CE QU'IL FAUT FAIRE?

In your opinion, what should be done to attain the following results? Use **il faut** and an expression of your choice.

▷ **Pour être dentiste,** *il faut aller à l'université (étudier la biologie...)* .

1. Pour être avocat, _____ .

2. Pour être chauffeur de taxi (*taxi driver*), _____ .

3. Pour maigrir, _____ .

4. Pour avoir des amis, _____ .

5. Pour être heureux (*happy*), _____ .

6. Pour bien parler français, _____ .

7. Pour avoir une profession intéressante, _____ .

TRADUCTION

Give the French equivalent of each of the following sentences.

1. *Do people speak French in Québec?*

   _____

2. *I want to go to the movies, but I can't.*

   _____

3. *In order to have an "A", one has to study.*

   _____

4. *My sister is a nurse, but she wants to be a doctor.*

   _____

POUR COMMUNIQUER   Vos projets

Describe your future plans: what you want to do this summer, what you want to do when you finish school, what career you would like to have. Describe what you have to do to reach these goals.

_____

_____

_____

_____

_____

_____

_____

_____

_____

UNITÉ 1   C'EST LA VIE!

Leçon 3   L'alibi

A1.   EXPRESSION PERSONNELLE

Say what you do under the following circumstances. Complete each of the sentences below with an expression of your choice.

▷   **Quand j'ai faim,** *je mange du chocolat (j'achète un sandwich, etc.)* .

1. Quand j'ai soif, _____ .

2. Quand j'ai chaud, _____ .

3. Quand j'ai froid, _____ .

4. Quand je n'ai pas sommeil, _____ .

5. Quand je n'ai pas envie d'étudier, _____ .

6. Quand j'ai envie de passer un week-end intéressant, _____ .

7. Quand j'ai besoin d'un conseil (*advice*), _____ .

8. Quand j'ai besoin d'argent, _____ .

B1.   ACHATS (*Purchases*)

The following students went shopping before leaving for vacation. Say what they chose, using the appropriate forms of the **passé composé** of **choisir.** Also say how much they paid, using the appropriate forms of the **passé composé** of **dépenser** and the indicated price.

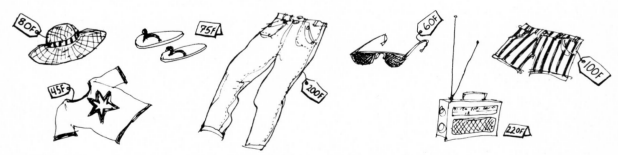

▷   **Henri** *a choisi* **deux shorts.** *Il a dépensé 200* francs.

1. Ève _____ des lunettes de soleil. _____ francs.

2. Nous _____ 3 tee-shirts. _____ francs.

3. Tu _____ un chapeau. _____ francs.

4. J'_____ 2 paires de sandales. _____ francs.

5. Mes amies _____ 2 paires de blue-jeans. _____ francs.

6. Vous _____ une radio. _____ francs.

B2.   OUI OU NON?

Read about the following people. Then say whether or not they have done the things in parentheses.

▷   **Paul est malade** (*sick*). **(regarder la télé? jouer au football?)**

Paul a regardé la télé. Il n'a pas joué au football.

1.   Nous jouons mal au tennis. (gagner? perdre?)

_____

2.   Philippe est un garçon très timide. (rougir? danser avec Catherine?)

_____

3.   Tu veux maigrir. (manger des frites? commander de l'eau minérale?)

_____

4.   Vous avez de la chance. (gagner à la loterie? perdre votre match?)

_____

5.   Je suis au régime (*on a diet*). (maigrir? grossir?)

_____

6.   Ces élèves sont consciencieux. (étudier? réussir à l'examen?)

_____

7.   Ces élèves ne sont pas consciencieux. (écouter le professeur? obéir?)

_____

C1.   L'ÉTÉ DERNIER

Read what the following people did last summer, and ask for more information about their activities. Complete each of the questions below, using a subject pronoun and *inversion*.

▷   **Jean-Paul a travaillé.**   Où   *a-t-il travaillé* _____ ?

1.   Jeannette a travaillé.   Pourquoi _____ ?

2.   André a visité Paris.   Quand _____ ?

3.   Mes cousins ont visité Québec.   Avec qui _____ ?

4.   Isabelle a vendu sa bicyclette. Pourquoi _____ ?

5.   Thérèse et Sylvie ont voyagé.   Avec qui _____ ?

POUR COMMUNIQUER   Une page de journal (*Page from a diary*)

Write about some of the things you did yesterday by answering the following questions in French.

1.   *What time did you have lunch? Where? What did you eat?* _____

_____

2.   *Did you play volleyball (or another sport)?* _____

_____

3.   *Did you visit a friend? Did you phone someone?* _____

_____

4.   *Did you watch TV? What programs did you watch?* _____

_____

Nom _____ Date _____

UNITÉ 1   C'EST LÀ VIE!
Leçon 4   Il n'y a pas de justice!

A1.   QU'EST-CE QU'ILS METTENT?

Read what the following young people are doing or want to do. Use this information to complete each of the sentences with the appropriate form of **mettre** and one of the items below.

   un disque / une belle robe / la télé / un pull / un maillot de bain / la table

1. Janine va à une boum élégante. Elle _____ .

2. J'ai envie d'écouter de la musique. Je _____ .

3. Vous allez dîner dans dix minutes. Vous _____ .

4. Tu vas à la plage. Tu _____ .

5. Nous voulons regarder le match de tennis. Nous _____ .

6. Mes cousins ont froid. Ils _____ .

B1.   QU'EST-CE QU'ILS FONT?

Read what the following people do or like to do. Then decide whether or not they did the things indicated in parentheses. Write out your responses, using the **passé composé** of **faire** in *affirmative* or *negative* sentences.

➪   **Mes cousins n'ont pas d'argent.**
   Cet été, *ils n'ont pas fait de voyage* _____ . (un voyage?)

1. Vous jouez mal.
   Vous _____ . (des progrès?)

2. Hélène arrive du supermarché.
   _____ . (les courses?)

3. Jacques aime aider (*to help*) sa mère.
   _____ . (la vaisselle?)

4. Tu n'aides pas ta mère.
   _____ . (le ménage?)

5. Nous n'allons jamais à l'hôtel.
   Cet été, _____ . (du camping?)

6. Oh là là! Il pleut!
   Pierre _____ aujourd'hui. (une promenade?)

7. J'aime jouer aux cartes (*cards*).
   _____ de bridge avec mes amis. (une partie?)

8. Mon père est un excellent cuisinier (*cook*).
   Dimanche, _____ . (la cuisine?)

B2. CONTENTS OU PAS?

Say what the following people did last weekend. Fill in the first blank of each item with the appropriate **passé composé** form of the verb in parentheses. Then say whether these people were happy or not. Use the **passé composé** of **être content** in an *affirmative* or *negative* sentence.

▷ (avoir)   Mes cousines _ont eu_ un accident.
    Elles n'ont pas été contentes! _____

1. (avoir)   Paul _____ un rendez-vous (*date*) avec Stéphanie.
    _____

2. (avoir)   J'_____ des problèmes avec mes parents.
    _____

3. (être)   Jeanne _____ au cinéma avec son meilleur ami.
    _____

4. (être)   Vous _____ malades (*sick*).
    _____

5. (boire)   Pour son anniversaire, M. Bertrand _____ du champagne avec ses amis.
    _____

6. (conduire)   Tu _____ la Mercédès de ton oncle.
    _____

7. (prendre)   Robert _____ d'excellentes photos.
    _____

8. (devoir)   Les élèves _____ préparer l'examen de maths.
    _____

9. (pouvoir)   Vous _____ aller au restaurant avec vos amis.
    _____

POUR COMMUNIQUER   Une page de journal

Write about some of the things you did yesterday by answering the following questions in French.

1. *Did you make your bed?* _____

2. *Did you do the dishes?* _____

3. *Did you have to study after dinner?* _____
    _____

4. *Were you able to go to the movies?* _____
    _____

UNITÉ 1 C'EST LA VIE!

Leçon 5 Ici tout va bien!

A1. SAMEDI SOIR

On Saturday night Philippe and his friends are going out. Complete each sentence with the appropriate forms of **sortir** and **partir**.

▷ Philippe _sort_ avec ses amis. Il _part_ après le dîner.

1. Hélène _____ avec Paul. Elle _____ à huit heures.

2. Suzanne et Monique _____ en ville. Elles _____ à sept heures.

3. Nous _____ avec des amies. Nous _____ avant le dîner.

4. Vous _____ avec Charles. Vous _____ à six heures.

5. Je _____ avec Marc. Je _____ à huit heures et demie.

6. Tu _____ avec Irène. Quand _____-tu?

B1. SENTIMENTS (*Feelings*)

The way we feel is often determined by what we have just done. Imagine how the people below feel and explain why. Use elements of columns A, B, and C, and the construction **venir de** in logical sentences.

A	B	C
content	gagner	un «A» / un «F»
triste	perdre	une longue promenade à pied / en voiture
fatigué	faire	le match de tennis / de rugby
malade (*sick*)	sortir avec	des amis sympathiques
	manger	des personnes stupides / amusantes
	avoir	un kilo de chocolat

▷ Pierre _est triste. Il vient d'avoir un "F"._

1. Nous _____

2. Tu _____

3. Paul et Jacques _____

4. Mélanie _____

5. Vous _____

6. Je _____

Unité un **39**

C1. LE WEEK-END DERNIER

Say what the following people did last weekend. Complete the first sentence of each item with the appropriate **passé composé** form of the verb in parentheses. Then use this information to say where they went. In your second sentence, use the **passé composé** of **aller** and one of the following places:

la piscine / le stade / la bibliothèque / le restaurant / la campagne / la discothèque

▷ (jouer) Olivier _a joué_ au football. _Il est allé au stade._

1. (nager) Monique _____ . _____

2. (déjeuner) Lise et Ève _____ avec des amis. _____

3. (regarder) Sylvie _____ des magazines. _____

4. (faire) Nous _____ du camping. _____

5. (danser) Vous _____ . _____

C2. HIER?

Say what happened or did not happen to the following people yesterday. Write a short paragraph for each person using the **passé composé** of the verbs in parentheses in either *affirmative* or *negative* sentences. (Be careful! Some of the verbs are conjugated with **être** and others with **avoir**.)

1. je (rester à la maison / arriver à l'heure [*on time*] à l'école / rentrer à midi chez moi)

   _Je (ne) suis (pas) resté(e) à la maison. Je _____

   _____

2. mon meilleur ami (téléphoner / venir chez moi)

   _____

   _____

3. mon père (prendre la voiture / rentrer dans une autre [*other*] voiture / aller à l'hôpital)

   _____

   _____

4. ma mère (sortir / tomber dans la rue [*street*])

   _____

5. le chat des voisins (entrer chez nous / monter sur le toit [*roof*])

   _____

POUR COMMUNIQUER   Une page de journal

Write about what you did last Friday by answering the following questions in French.

1. *What time did you arrive at school?* _____

2. *How many hours did you stay there?* _____

3. *What time did you get home?* _____

4. *Did you go out? With whom?* _____

Récréation culturelle

Vive le sport!

Voici la liste de quelques sports des Jeux Olympiques d'été. Examinez cette liste et indiquez par une croix (X) les sports que vous pratiquez (*play, take part in*), les sports que vous regardez à la télévision et les sports que vous aimeriez (*would like*) pratiquer.

	je pratique ce sport	je regarde ce sport à la télé	j'aimerais pratiquer ce sport
athlétisme			
aviron			
basketball			
cyclisme			
football			
gymnastique			
hockey			
natation			
voile			
volleyball			

1. Quel est votre sport individuel préféré (*favorite*)? _____

    Quand et où pratiquez-vous ce sport? _____

    _____

    Avec qui? _____

2. Quel est votre sport d'équipe préféré? _____

    Quand, où et avec qui pratiquez-vous ce sport? _____

    _____

Unité 1

Récréation culturelle

Petit déjeuner au Frontenac

Imaginez que vous visitez Québec. Vous êtes logé(e) au Château Frontenac, le plus grand hôtel de la ville. C'est l'heure du petit déjeuner. Aujourd'hui vous avez très faim. Lisez le menu et indiquez votre choix (*choice*) dans le tableau (*board*).

Le Château Frontenac

(De 06h30 à 11h00)   (06h30 to 11h00)

LE CONTINENTAL $5.80

☐ **Jus d'orange**   ☐ Orange juice

☐ **Café ou**   ☐ Coffee or
☐ **thé ou**   ☐ tea or
☐ **lait**   ☐ milk

　　avec croissant, brioche,　　with croissant, brioche,
　　beurre et confiture　　　　butter and preserve

LE FRONTENAC $10.50

☐ **Jus de pamplemousse ou**   ☐ Grapefruit juice or
☐ **jus d'orange ou**   ☐ orange juice or
☐ **jus de tomate ou**   ☐ tomato juice or
☐ **demi-pamplemousse ou**   ☐ half grapefruit or
☐ **pruneaux**   ☐ stewed prunes

☐ **Jambon ou**   ☐ Ham or
☐ **bacon ou**   ☐ bacon or
☐ **saucisses**   ☐ sausages

☐ **Deux oeufs frits ou**   ☐ Two fried eggs or
☐ **oeufs brouillés ou**   ☐ scrambled eggs or
☐ **deux oeufs à la coque**   ☐ two boiled eggs

☐ **Café ou**   ☐ Coffee or
☐ **thé ou**   ☐ tea or
☐ **lait**   ☐ milk

　　avec rôties,　　　　　with toast,
　　beurre et confiture　　butter and preserve

---

jus de fruits:

_____

_____

viande:

_____

_____

œufs:

_____

_____

boissons:

_____

_____

Récréation culturelle

Déjeuner à Québec

À midi vous déjeunez dans un restaurant de Québec. Regardez le menu et marquez par une croix (X) les plats que vous connaissez.

Cuisine Québécoise

Les Entrées:
Fondue Parmesan
Oeufs mayonnaise
Fèves au lard

Les Potages:
Consommé
Soupe
Jus de tomates

Les Salades:
Salade de poulet
Salade aux oeufs
Salade du chef

Les petits hors-d'oeuvre

Ragoût de Pattes et Boulettes
Pâté à la viande et salade de patates
Vol au vent au poulet
Omelette
Tourtière "Saguenéenne"
Entrecôte Marchand de vin
Brochette de boeuf
Filet mignon

Desserts:
Trempette à la crème et sucre d'érable

À la crêperie

Crêperie - Restaurant
de la Perchais
~~~~~~~

Spécialités de :
Crêpes sucrées et salées
Omelettes _ Mets divers
Coupes glacées

GLOSSAIRE: **salées** *salted* **Mets divers** *Various dishes*
Coupes glacées *Ice cream*

Regardez cette publicité (*advertisement*) et répondez aux questions ci-dessous (*below*).

1. Avez-vous déjà (*ever*) mangé des crêpes?

   _____

2. En principe quelle est la spécialité d'une «crêperie»?

   _____

3. Quels sont les autres (*other*) plats offerts (*offered*) par cette crêperie?

   _____

Dîner à Paris

Imaginez que vous êtes à Paris. Aujourd'hui vous visitez le Quartier Latin, qui est le quartier des étudiants. Vous décidez de dîner au «Luxembourg», un restaurant assez bon marché. Choisissez votre menu et écrivez votre choix dans la case ci-dessous (*box below*). Indiquez le prix de chaque plat et faites l'addition (*add up the check*).

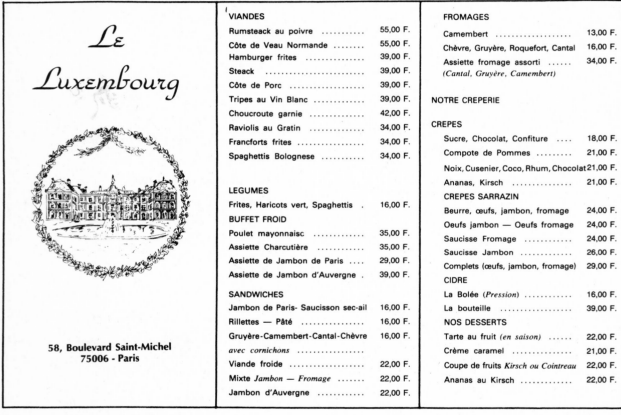

Le Luxembourg

58, Boulevard Saint-Michel
75006 - Paris

VIANDES

Rumsteack au poivre	55,00 F.
Côte de Veau Normande	55,00 F.
Hamburger frites	39,00 F.
Steack	39,00 F.
Côte de Porc	39,00 F.
Tripes au Vin Blanc	39,00 F.
Choucroute garnie	42,00 F.
Raviolis au Gratin	34,00 F.
Francforts frites	34,00 F.
Spaghettis Bolognese	34,00 F.

LEGUMES

Frites, Haricots vert, Spaghettis	16,00 F.

BUFFET FROID

Poulet mayonnaisc	35,00 F.
Assiette Charcutière	35,00 F.
Assiette de Jambon de Paris	29,00 F.
Assiette de Jambon d'Auvergne	39,00 F.

SANDWICHES

Jambon de Paris- Saucisson sec-ail	16,00 F.
Rillettes — Pâté	16,00 F.
Gruyère-Camembert-Cantal-Chèvre	16,00 F.
avec cornichons	
Viande froide	22,00 F.
Mixte *Jambon — Fromage*	22,00 F.
Jambon d'Auvergne	22,00 F.

FROMAGES

Camembert	13,00 F.
Chèvre, Gruyère, Roquefort, Cantal	16,00 F.
Assiette fromage assorti	34,00 F.
(Cantal, Gruyère, Camembert)	

NOTRE CREPERIE

CREPES

Sucre, Chocolat, Confiture	18,00 F.
Compote de Pommes	21,00 F.
Noix, Cusenier, Coco, Rhum, Chocolat	21,00 F.
Ananas, Kirsch	21,00 F.

CREPES SARRAZIN

Beurre, œufs, jambon, fromage	24,00 F.
Oeufs jambon — Oeufs fromage	24,00 F.
Saucisse Fromage	24,00 F.
Saucisse Jambon	26,00 F.
Complets (œufs, jambon, fromage)	29,00 F.

CIDRE

La Bolée (*Pression*)	16,00 F.
La bouteille	39,00 F.

NOS DESSERTS

Tarte au fruit (*en saison*)	22,00 F.
Crème caramel	21,00 F.
Coupe de fruits *Kirsch ou Cointreau*	22,00 F.
Ananas au Kirsch	22,00 F.

1. Êtes-vous déjà (*ever*) allé(e) dans un restaurant français? Où? Quand? Avec qui? Qu'est-ce que vous avez mangé? Qu'est-ce que vous avez bu?

   _____

   _____

   _____

   _____

2. Quels sont vos plats favoris?

   _____

   _____

MON MENU

plat	prix
_____	_____
_____	_____
_____	_____
total:	_____

Récréation culturelle

Les fromages de France

La France est un pays réputé (*well-known*) pour ses fromages. Il existe 400 variétés de fromages. Chaque région a ses spécialités. Voici quelques (*a few*) fromages français.

LE CAMEMBERT: C'est un fromage rond, originaire de Normandie.

LE BRIE: Ce fromage ressemble au camembert. Il est fabriqué dans la Brie, une région située (*located*) à l'est de Paris.

LE MUNSTER: C'est un fromage originaire d'Alsace.

LE ROQUEFORT: Ce fromage a une saveur (*flavor*) assez forte (*strong*). Il est fabriqué dans les caves de Roquefort-sur-Soulzon, dans le sud de la France.

UNITÉ 2: *Jim*

INTRODUCTION: What you will do and learn in *Unité 2*

LESSON OPENERS

In this unit (and in all the units to follow) the five lesson openers form a continuous story. In *Unité 2* Marc and Nicole, two French students, are waiting for the arrival of Jim, their American pen pal, who is going to spend his vacation in Europe. They have never met him and are very anxious to see what he looks like . . .

NOTES CULTURELLES

You will learn about American cities with French names, about the old and the new Paris, and about the attitudes of young French people toward American culture.

ACTIVITÉS

This is the last unit in which you will mainly practice the communication skills you learned last year, especially how

pages in your textbook

to say that you know people, places, or things 130–131
to say that you never did certain things 144

You will also practice some *new* communication skills, especially how

to describe personal characteristics 143
to say that you no longer do certain things 144

STRUCTURE

You will continue to review some important aspects of French grammar, especially direct and indirect object pronouns, *savoir* vs. *connaître*, and the verbs *dire*, *lire*, *écrire*, and *voir*. You will also learn several new structures, including the relative pronouns *qui* and *que*, irregular adjectives, and the negative expression *ne . . . plus* (not . . . anymore).

UNITÉ 2   JIM

Leçon 1   Une lettre des États-Unis

A1.   À LA BIBLIOTHÈQUE

The following people are at the library. Read the descriptions, and say whether the people are *reading* or *writing*.

▷ **Philippe a un livre.**   *Il lit.* _____

1. Tu utilises un crayon. _____
2. Vous avez un magazine. _____
3. Nous avons nos stylos. _____
4. Paul et Pierre regardent les journaux. _____
5. Je prends du papier. _____
6. Ces garçons ont leurs crayons. _____
7. Cette fille prend une enveloppe et du papier. _____
8. Tu regardes le journal. _____

A2.   UN DÉBAT SUR LA PERCEPTION EXTRA-SENSORIELLE (*A debate about ESP*)

Does ESP exist? A group of friends are debating the question. Give everyone's opinion, using the appropriate forms of **dire**.

▷ **Nicole / oui**   *Nicole dit que oui.* _____

1. Georges / non _____
2. je / c'est possible _____
3. mes cousins / c'est vrai _____
4. nous / c'est une idée ridicule _____
5. vous / c'est impossible _____
6. tu / tu n'es pas sûr _____

B1.   RELATIONS PERSONNELLES

Describe your relationship with the following people. Use the suggested verbs in *affirmative* or *negative* sentences. Use the pronoun **me (m')** in sentences 1-4, and the pronoun **nous** in sentences 5-8.

1. Mes parents _____. (comprendre)
2. Mon oncle _____. (écrire)
3. Mon meilleur ami _____. (admirer)
4. Les élèves de la classe _____. (téléphoner)
5. Nos professeurs _____. (encourager)
6. Les adultes _____. (comprendre)
7. Le président _____. (promettre des réformes)
8. Les journalistes _____. (dire la vérité)

B2. RÉCIPROCITÉ

Reciprocity requires that if you do something for a friend, this friend agrees to do *the same thing* for you. Express this idea according to the model. (Be sure that the verb agrees with the new subject.)

▷ **Tu téléphones à Marie.**   Marie *te téléphone* _____.

1. Tu écris à Daniel.   Daniel _____.

2. Je dis la vérité à Marc.   Marc _____.

3. Nous répondons à Jacques.   Jacques _____.

4. Vous invitez ces filles.   Ces filles _____.

5. Je t'invite.   Tu _____.

C1. OUI ET NON

Paul wants his cousin Annette to do certain things for him. He does not want his cousins Louis and Henri to do the same things. Write what Paul tells them.

          à Annette: **à Louis et à Henri:**

▷ (téléphoner)   *Téléphone-moi!*   *Ne me téléphonez pas!*

1. (inviter) _____   _____

2. (parler de tes / vos amis) _____   _____

3. (attendre) _____   _____

4. (écrire) _____   _____

5. (répondre) _____   _____

D1. PROMESSES (*Promises*)

The first person in each of the situations below has promised the other ones to do something for them. Write out each person's promise, using the construction **aller** + *infinitive*.

▷ **Alain / à nous / écrire**   *Alain va nous écrire.* _____

1. mes cousins / à moi / inviter _____

2. Sylvie / à vous / répondre _____

3. nous / à toi / attendre _____

4. le professeur / à nous / parler _____

5. tu / à moi / conduire à la plage _____

POUR COMMUNIQUER   Relations personnelles

Answer the following questions in French.

1. *Does your best friend listen to you?* _____

2. *Do your parents understand you?* _____

3. *Do your grandparents write you often?* _____

4. *Are your cousins going to invite you this summer?* _____

UNITÉ 2   JIM
Leçon 2   Qui est Jim?

A1.   QU'EST-CE QU'ILS VOIENT?

Read where the people below are or went. Say which of the following things they are seeing (sentences 1–6) or they have seen (sentences 7–9). Use the *present* or the **passé composé** of **voir.**

un western / des avions / des oiseaux / un éléphant / une comédie musicale /
des sculptures / la tour Eiffel / les Expos / les Red Sox

1.   Mes parents sont à Paris. _____

2.   Je suis au musée. _____

3.   Tu es à l'aéroport. _____

4.   Nous sommes à la campagne. _____

5.   Vous êtes au zoo. _____

6.   Mon cousin est au cinéma. _____

7.   Nous sommes allés à Montréal. _____

8.   Ma sœur est allée au théâtre. _____

9.   Vous êtes allés à Boston. _____

B1.   CONNAISSANCES (*Acquaintances*)

Complete each of the following sentences with the appropriate form of **connaître.** Note that sentences 1–4 may be *affirmative* or *negative*.

1.   Ma mère _____ Paris.

2.   Mes parents _____ mes professeurs.

3.   Nous _____ bien nos voisins.

4.   Je _____ les cousins de mon meilleur ami.

5.   Est-ce que tu _____ des Français?

6.   Est-ce que vous _____ ce restaurant?

C1.   RÉACTIONS

Read about the following people, and say what they do for their friends and acquaintances. Use the verbs in parentheses in *affirmative* or *negative* sentences. Use a *direct object pronoun* when referring to the people mentioned in italics.

1.   Henri aime *Catherine*. (voir souvent? trouver sympathique? oublier?)

Il la voit souvent. Il _____

2.   J'ai *deux cousines* au Japon. (inviter souvent? voir souvent?)

_____

3.   Les élèves trouvent *le professeur* intéressant. (écouter? comprendre? critiquer?)

_____

C2. SUGGESTIONS

A French friend has asked you what you think about certain people and things. Your opinions are expressed below. Tell your friend to act accordingly. Use the *imperative* of the verbs in parentheses in *affirmative* or *negative* commands. Use the appropriate *direct object pronouns*.

▷ Ce livre est assez intéressant. (lire?) *Lis-le!*

1. Ce disque est excellent. (écouter?) _____

2. Cette revue est très intéressante. (lire?) _____

3. Ces exercices sont très difficiles. (faire?) _____

4. Ces garçons sont snobs. (inviter?) _____

5. Ces garçons ne sont pas ponctuels. (attendre?) _____

6. Cette fille dit des mensonges. (écouter?) _____

D1. HIER

Say whether or not you saw the following people yesterday. Use a *direct object pronoun* and the **passé composé** of **voir**.

▷ votre meilleur ami? *Je l'ai vu. (Je ne l'ai pas vu.)*

1. votre cousin? _____

2. vos voisins? _____

3. votre grand-mère? _____

4. le facteur (*mailman*)? _____

5. les sœurs de votre meilleur ami? _____

D2. ACCUSATIONS

Monique accuses her sister Nicole of having done the following things. Nicole says that she has not done them. Write her replies.

Monique: Nicole:

▷ **Tu as lu mes lettres!** *Non, je ne les ai pas lues.*

1. Tu as lu mon carnet! _____

2. Tu as écouté mes disques! _____

3. Tu as pris ma calculatrice! _____

4. Tu as pris mes lunettes de soleil! _____

5. Tu as perdu mon stylo! _____

6. Tu as conduit ma voiture! _____

POUR COMMUNIQUER Questions

Answer the following questions in French, using *object pronouns*.

1. *Do you know your neighbors well?* _____

2. *Do you often see your cousins?* _____

3. *Did you help your mother yesterday?* _____

4. *Did you meet your friends last night* (**hier soir**)? _____

UNITÉ 2   JIM

Leçon 3   Un garçon timide et fatigué

A1.   DOMMAGE! (*Too bad!*)

The following people are not doing certain things because they do not know how. Express this by using **savoir** + *infinitive*.

▷ **Henri ne conduit pas.**   *Il ne sait pas conduire.*

1.   Jacqueline ne nage pas. _____

2.   Philippe et Raymond ne dansent pas. _____

3.   Vous ne parlez pas espagnol. _____

4.   Tu ne fais pas la cuisine. _____

5.   Je ne chante pas. _____

6.   Nous ne skions pas. _____

A2.   MARIE-FRANÇOISE

Marie-Françoise is a new student. Say that the following people know certain things about her by completing each of the sentences below with the appropriate form of **connaître** or **savoir**.

1.   Le professeur _____ ses parents.

2.   Tu _____ où elle habite.

3.   Nous _____ sa cousine.

4.   Vous _____ avec qui elle sort.

5.   Nathalie _____ qu'elle est sympathique.

6.   Jeanne et Henri _____ les amis de son frère.

7.   Je _____ que ses cousins l'invitent souvent.

B1.   JOYEUX ANNIVERSAIRE! (*Happy birthday!*)

Imagine that the following people are celebrating their birthdays this month. Read about their preferences, and then say what you are going to give them. Use the appropriate *indirect object pronoun* . . . and your imagination.

▷ **Paul aime la musique classique.**   *Je lui donne un disque de Mozart.*

1.   Françoise aime les animaux. _____

2.   Sylvie est une fille très élégante. _____

3.   Albert et Henri jouent au tennis. _____

4.   Anne et Suzanne aiment bien manger. _____

5.   Robert aime lire. _____

B2. RAPPORTS PERSONNELS (*Personal relationships*)

Read about the following people. Then say what they do for their friends. Use the verbs in parentheses in *affirmative* or *negative* sentences. Also use the appropriate *direct* or *indirect object pronouns*.

1. Paul a un très bon ami en Australie. (téléphoner souvent? écrire? voir souvent?)

   Il *ne lui téléphone pas souvent. Il* _____

   _____

2. Nathalie respecte ses parents. (obéir? écouter? dire des mensonges?)

   Elle _____

   _____

3. Vous avez une amie qui est très indiscrète. (parler de vos problèmes? montrer vos photos? inviter chez vous?)

   Vous _____

   _____

4. J'ai des cousines qui sont très sympathiques mais qui perdent tout. (rendre visite? inviter? prêter vos disques?)

   Je _____

   _____

B3. DÉJÀ FAIT! (*Already done!*)

Marc tells Claire what he is going to do. Claire tells him that she has already done these things. Complete Claire's sentences. Be sure to use the **passé composé.**

Marc:

▷ **Je vais parler à Henri.**

1. Je vais parler au professeur.
2. Je vais rendre visite à Hélène.
3. Je vais téléphoner à Paul et à André.
4. Je vais téléphoner à Lise et à Marie.

Claire:

Moi, je lui ai parlé _____ hier.

_____ jeudi.

_____ dimanche.

_____ ce matin.

_____ à 9 heures.

POUR COMMUNIQUER   Questions personnelles

Answer the following questions in French.

1. *Do you know where the teacher lives?* _____

2. *Do you often phone your cousins?* _____

3. *Did you phone your uncle yesterday?* _____

   _____

4. *Did you visit your grandparents last weekend?* _____

   _____

UNITÉ 2 JIM
Leçon 4 Une mauvaise journée

A1. JACQUES ET JULES

Jacques and Jules have two very different impressions of Paris. Jacques lives in a neighborhood where everything is *old*, and Jules lives in an area where everything is *new*. Complete Jacques's account with the appropriate forms of **vieux**. Then write the corresponding account made by Jules, using the appropriate forms of **nouveau**.

JACQUES: J'habite un ___*vieux*___ quartier. Dans ce quartier, il y a un _____ théâtre,

un _____ hôtel, une _____ église, des _____ maisons et

des _____ monuments.

JULES: J'habite ___*un nouveau quartier. Dans*___ _____

_____

_____

B1. IDENTIFICATIONS

The following paragraph tells what certain students are doing in the classroom as the substitute teacher enters. She asks Pierre to identify his classmates. Write out what Pierre says, starting your sentences with **C'est le garçon (la fille) qui** or **Ce sont les garçons (les filles) qui.**

Jacques lit. Michèle regarde sa montre. Philippe mange un sandwich. Françoise écrit. André et Gilles parlent. Christine et Mathilde lisent leurs livres. Irène et Marie sortent.

le professeur: **Pierre:**

▷ **Qui sont Irène et Marie?**   *Ce sont les filles qui sortent.*

1. Qui est Jacques? _____

2. Qui est Michèle? _____

3. Qui est Philippe? _____

4. Qui est Françoise? _____

5. Qui sont André et Gilles? _____

6. Qui sont Christine et Mathilde? _____

B2. EXPRESSION PERSONNELLE

Complete each of the sentences below with an expression of your choice.

▷ J'ai un ami qui ___*a un cousin français (a visité Paris, etc.)*___ .

1. J'ai une amie qui _____ .

2. J'ai des parents qui _____ .

3. Mes parents ont une voiture qui _____ .

4. Nous habitons dans une maison qui _____ .

5. Paris est une ville qui _____ .

C1. ET VOUS?

Nicole is telling you what she does or what she likes. Say whether or not you do or like the same things. Follow the model.

	Nicole:	vous:
⇨	J'aime New York.	C'est une ville *que j'aime (que je n'aime pas)*.
1.	Je connais San Francisco.	C'est une ville _____ .
2.	Je lis «*Time* magazine».	C'est une revue _____ .
3.	J'admire le président des États-Unis.	C'est un homme _____ .
4.	Je trouve Woody Allen très drôle.	C'est un comédien _____ .
5.	J'écoute souvent les «Rolling Stones».	Ce sont des musiciens _____ .

C2. MAUDITE PLUIE! (*Darned rain!*)

Daniel left his homework outside when he went to play baseball. It started raining. When Daniel got back, he noticed that the words **qui** and **que** had been washed away. Put them back.

1. La jeune fille _____ Paul regarde est très sympathique. C'est une Américaine _____ vient passer une année à Paris.

2. Je donne une boum pour les personnes _____ aiment danser et _____ j'aime bien.

3. J'ai un ami _____ vous ne connaissez pas mais _____ connaît votre sœur.

4. La personne _____ vous cherchez n'est pas là. Demandez son adresse à la dame _____ est là-bas.

5. La Renault _____ est devant le café est la voiture _____ je viens d'acheter.

6. Voici le journal _____ je lis. C'est un journal _____ est idiot.

TRADUCTION

Give the French equivalent of each of the following sentences.

1. *I live in a house that has a very old garage* (**un garage**).

   _____

2. *I do not like the book that you are reading.*

   _____

3. *Anne is inviting a girl whom we do not know.*

   _____

4. *My cousin has friends who live in Saint Louis.*

   _____

POUR COMMUNIQUER   Vos préférences

Describe the people and things you like or do not like. Complete the sentences below with **qui** or **que** and an expression of your choice.

1. J'aime les gens _____ .

2. Je n'aime pas les gens _____ .

3. J'aime les livres _____ .

4. J'aime les magazines _____ .

5. Je n'aime pas les films _____ .

UNITÉ 2 JIM
Leçon 5 Il y a plus d'un Jim en Amérique

A1. LE RAPPORT DU PROFESSEUR LEJUMELÉ

In a scientific treatise, the famous professor Lejumelé shows that twins have identical character traits. Here is part of his evidence. Complete it by describing the twin girl in each pair.

1. Joël est attentif, bon et généreux.

    Joëlle est _attentive,_ _____ .

2. Charles est ambitieux et original.

    Charlotte est _____ .

3. Martin est ponctuel et actif.

    Martine est _____ .

4. Louis est intuitif et musicien.

    Louise est _____ .

5. Noël est naïf, superstitieux et irrationnel.

    Noëlle est _____ .

A2. OUI OU NON?

Read about the following people. Then describe them in *affirmative* or *negative* sentences, using the appropriate forms of the adjectives in parentheses. (These adjectives are given in the *masculine singular* form.)

 Virginie et Stéphanie sont des championnes de tennis. (sportif?)

   Elles sont sportives. _____

1. Bernard et Louis travaillent beaucoup. (paresseux?)

    _____

2. François et André ont des idées brillantes. (original?)

    _____

3. Claire et Nadine aident leurs amies. (loyal?)

    _____

4. Isabelle et Francine sont contentes. (malheureux?)

    _____

5. Thérèse et Jeannette sont jolies. (mignon?)

    _____

B1. UNE QUESTION DE PERSONNALITÉ (*A matter of personality*)

Describe the personalities of the people below, choosing an expression from column A. Then say what these people never do, by using a verb from column B in a *negative* sentence with **jamais**.

A	B
sincère	travailler
paresseux	attendre
impatient	danser
timide	dire des mensonges
loyal	critiquer (ses) amis
bon élève	avoir un «F»
actif	perdre (son) temps

▷ Jacqueline *est sincère. Elle ne dit jamais de mensonges.*

1. Vous _____

2. Nous _____

3. Mélanie _____

4. Je _____

5. Anne et Suzanne _____

6. Tu _____

B2. LA PREMIÈRE FOIS (*The first time*)

This summer the following people are going to do something they have never done before. Express this, using the **passé composé** and **ne . . . jamais**.

▷ **Philippe va visiter Tahiti.** *Il n'a jamais visité Tahiti.*

1. Valérie va prendre l'avion. _____

2. Tu vas aller au Mexique. _____

3. Je vais faire de la planche à voile. _____

4. Vous allez faire de l'alpinisme. _____

5. Nous allons voir Bruxelles. _____

6. Mon frère va conduire. _____

7. Henri va monter à la tour Eiffel. _____

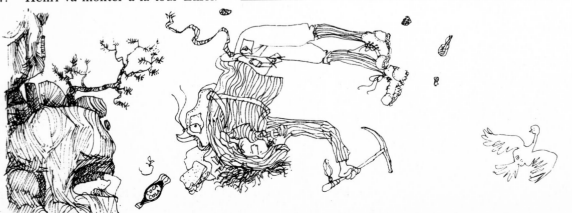

B3.   ANNETTE A LA GRIPPE (*Annette has the flu*)

Annette, who is in bed with the flu, cannot see anyone or do anything. When Philippe phones her, she answers all his questions negatively. Write her replies, using the *present tense* in items 1–4 and the **passé composé** in items 5–8. Be sure to use the appropriate *negative* expression.

Philippe: **Annette:**

1.   Tu fais quelque chose?   _____

2.   Tu attends quelqu'un?   _____

3.   Tu regardes quelque chose à la télé?   _____

4.   Tu veux quelque chose?   _____

5.   Tu as parlé à quelqu'un?   _____

6.   Tu as mangé quelque chose?   _____

7.   Tu as bu quelque chose?   _____

TRADUCTION

Give the French equivalent of each of the following sentences.

1.   *I never work on Sundays.*

_____

2.   *Robert does not travel because he does not have his car anymore.*

_____

3.   *We have never visited this museum.*

_____

4.   *I heard something, but I did not see anyone.*

_____

POUR COMMUNIQUER Rêves (*Dreams*)

Describe six things you would like to do but that you have never done.

▷   *Je voudrais aller au Canada. Je ne suis jamais allé(e) au Canada.*

Récréation culturelle

Joyeux anniversaire!

Regardez la carte d'anniversaire et répondez aux questions suivantes.

1. Comment s'appelle la personne qui célèbre son anniversaire?

   _____

2. Comment s'appelle la personne qui lui a écrit cette carte?

   _____

GLOSSAIRE: **vœux** *wishes* **avenir** *future* **tout entier** *whole*

Chère Barbara,
Heureux Anniversaire
et
Meilleurs Vœux
Claude.

En cet Heureux Anniversaire
Le temps ne compte pas
L'avenir tout entier est là.

Composez en français une petite carte pour l'anniversaire de votre meilleur(e) ami(e).

Unité 2

Joyeux Noël!

À Noël les élèves français ont deux semaines de vacances. Pendant ces vacances, un grand nombre de jeunes vont faire du ski dans les Alpes ou les Pyrénées.

Noël est aussi l'occasion de réunions familiales. C'est aussi l'époque (*time*) où on envoie (*sends*) les «cartes de vœux» (*greeting cards*) à ses amis. Regardez les cartes de Noël.

BONNE
FÊTE
DE
NOËL

Noël, c'est la joie
de redécouvrir
le sapin touffu et
les guirlandes argentées.

C'est aussi
le visage épanoui
d'un enfant
qui attend.

JOYEUX
NOËL!

Hallmark Cards, Inc.

GLOSSAIRE: **sapin** *fir tree* **touffu** *bushy* **guirlandes** *garlands, chains*
argentées *silvery* **visage** *face* **épanoui** *beaming*

JOYEUX NOËL

Joyeux Noël
Sincères vœux
de Bonne Année
Bonne Santé
bonheur et prospérité

1. Comment dit-on «Merry Christmas»?

_____

2. Comment dit-on «Happy New Year»?

_____

3. Est-ce que vous envoyez des «cartes de vœux» pour la nouvelle année?

_____

À qui? _____

_____

_____

GLOSSAIRE: **santé** *health* **bonheur** *happiness*

Récréation culturelle

Petites annonces

Le Minitel est un service offert par la compagnie française de téléphone. C'est un réseau (*network*) sur ordinateur qui permet de faire des réservations, d'obtenir toutes sortes d'informations et de lire et d'écrire des petites annonces.

Ici, le magazine pour jeunes **Podium** offre un service de correspondance. Voici quelques (*a few*) annonces:

LES PETITES ANNONCES SUR MINITEL

ACHATS VENTES

Cherche tout sur Madonna: photos, autographes, posters, T-shirts—tout. Merci beaucoup. Sophie Boulogne, 1, avenue des Vergers, 72100 Le Mans.

Désire documents, photos et posters sur River Phoenix, Rob Lowe et Dépêche-Mode. Possibilités d'échange. Jean-Marc Ponte, 276, bd la Madeleine, 06000 Nice.

Je collectionne photos et cartes postales des États-Unis. Nathalie Gausselan, 128, rue Riolan, 80000 Amiens.

S.O.S AMITIÉ

J'ai 14 ans et je désire correspondre avec des filles ou des garçons entre 14 et 16 ans. J'aime le sport, le tennis et les chanteurs rock. Inclure une photo. Marie Violeau, 37, rue de la Messe, 45000 Orléans.

J'ai 15 ans et je veux correspondre avec des filles ou des garçons parlant l'anglais. Mes chanteurs préférés sont Madonna, Indochine, Sabrina et Samantha Fox. Florence Rondeau, 14, rue de Lausanne, 48300 St-Louis.

Bonjour à vous tous. J'ai 15 ans et demi et je veux correspondre avec des filles de mon âge. J'aime la musique moderne et les animaux. Daniel Gallet, 4, rue de la Monnaie, 54000 Nancy.

GLOSSAIRE: **achats** *purchases*   **ventes** *sales*   **amitié** *friendship*

Maintenant, écrivez votre propre offre de vente et une offre de correspondance.

UNITÉ 3: *Le mariage de Jacqueline*

INTRODUCTION: What you will do and learn in *Unité 3*

LESSON OPENERS

Jacqueline Lefèvre and Louis Jacomme are about to get married. You will read about their wedding day and find out why the ceremony did not go quite as smoothly as they had planned.

NOTES CULTURELLES

You will learn about French marriage customs, especially the engagement, the wedding ceremony, and the wedding feast. You will also learn about French attitudes toward being on time.

ACTIVITÉS

You will practice some important new communication skills, especially how

pages in your textbook

STRUCTURE

You will mainly learn reflexive verbs, which are verbs that use reflexive pronouns. You will also learn the verbs *appeler* (to call) and *recevoir* (to receive), and the adjective *tout* (all, every). In addition you will review the verbs *acheter* and *espérer*.

UNITÉ 3 LE MARIAGE DE JACQUELINE

Leçon 1 Derniers préparatifs

VI. ARCHITECTURE

Imagine that you are working in an architect's office. Draw up the floor plans for two houses: one for a young married couple with no children, and the other for a family with three children (two boys and a girl). Label each room and feature.

la maison du jeune couple

la maison de la famille de 3 enfants

A1. SHOPPING

Read where the following people are going or have gone. Then say which items listed in the box below they are buying or have bought. Use **acheter** in the *present tense* (sentences 1–6) and in the **passé composé** (sentences 7–8).

1. Charles va à la poste. Il _____ .

2. Je vais à la pharmacie. J'_____ .

3. Nous allons à la librairie. Nous _____ .

4. Vous allez chez le marchand de fruits. Vous _____ .

5. Tu vas au supermarché. Tu _____ .

6. Mes cousines vont dans un magasin de vêtements. Elles _____ .

7. Nous sommes allés à l'agence Chevrolet. Nous _____ .

8. Mon frère est allé chez le marchand de motos. Il _____ .

des oranges	une Kawasaki
de la limonade	de l'aspirine
des tee-shirts	des timbres
des livres	une Nova

A2. LE VERBE JUSTE (*The correct verb*)

Fill in each of the sentences with the appropriate present tense form of the verb from the box that fits logically.

1. François a étudié. Il _____ avoir un «A» à l'examen.

2. Je n'aime pas les westerns. Je _____ les comédies.

3. Quand les élèves ne comprennent pas, le professeur _____ la question.

4. Philippe _____ sa fiancée à la boum.

5. Nous _____ qu'il va faire beau parce que nous voulons aller à la plage.

6. Est-ce que vous _____ votre frère au pique-nique?

amener
espérer
préférer
répéter

B1.C1. APRÈS LE MATCH DE FOOTBALL

After the football game, everyone feels hungry. Say what they are doing by filling in the appropriate *reflexive pronouns*.

1. Paul _____ fait un sandwich.

2. Jacques et Louis _____ préparent une omelette.

3. Nous _____ achetons un gâteau.

4. Vous _____ préparez un hamburger.

5. Tu _____ fais des œufs brouillés (*scrambled eggs*).

6. Je _____ achète du chocolat.

B2.C2. AVANT L'EXAMEN

There is an important exam tomorrow, but not everyone is studying for it. Read what the following people are doing, and say whether or not they are getting ready for the test. Use the appropriate forms of **se préparer** (*to get ready*) in *affirmative* or *negative* sentences.

▷ Anne regarde la télé.   *Elle ne se prépare pas.*

1. Robert étudie. _____

2. Je vais au cinéma. _____

3. Antoine et Pierre apprennent les verbes. _____

4. Nous sortons avec nos amis. _____

5. Claire et Lucie vont danser. _____

6. Tu es à la bibliothèque. _____

7. Vous dormez. _____

8. Roland et Thomas sont à la piscine. _____

B3.C3. SHOPPING

The people below are going shopping. Say that they are buying the first item in parentheses for themselves and the second item for the person who is accompanying them. Use the appropriate pronouns, as in the model.

▷ Gérard va à la librairie avec sa petite sœur. (un livre / des bandes dessinées)
   Il s'achète un livre. Il lui achète des bandes dessinées.

1. Thomas va à la bijouterie (*jewelry shop*) avec sa fiancée. (une bague / des boucles d'oreille)

_____

2. Madame Bernard va dans un magasin de vêtements avec ses enfants. (une robe / des pantalons)

_____

3. Je vais à la cafétéria avec mes cousins. (une glace / un Coca-Cola)

_____

4. Nous allons au supermarché avec Antoine. (du chocolat / du chewing-gum)

_____

TRADUCTION

Give the French equivalent of each of the following sentences.

1. *I am making myself a sandwich.*

   _____

2. *Thérèse is looking at herself in the mirror* (**la glace**).

   _____

3. *Pierre washed his car. Now, he is washing himself.*

   _____

4. *Are you getting ready for the exam* (**l'examen**)?

   _____

POUR COMMUNIQUER   L'argent de poche

Write six sentences describing on which items you spend your money and on which items you do not spend it. Use the verb **s'acheter.**

_____

_____

_____

_____

_____

_____

_____

UNITÉ 3   LE MARIAGE DE JACQUELINE
Leçon 2   Un absent

V1.   EN CLASSE

Look at the seating chart for the French class. Indicate the position of the first person in each pair in relation to the second person.

le professeur

Bernard   Isabelle   Thomas   Jean-Louis

Sylvie   René   Henri   Marc

Claude   Lucie   Marie   Annette

⇨ **Isabelle / Thomas**   *Isabelle est à côté de (à gauche de, près de) Thomas.*

1. René / Isabelle   _____

2. Claude / Jean-Louis   _____

3. le professeur / la classe   _____

4. Henri / Marc   _____

5. Marie / Lucie   _____

6. Marc / Annette   _____

7. Claude / Sylvie   _____

V2.A1. PHOTO DE FAMILLE

Imagine that you are a photographer taking a picture of the family below. Tell the six children where to place themselves in relation to the adults. Use the imperative forms of **se mettre** . . . and your own sense of artistic arrangement.

Papa   Maman   Oncle Bernard   Tante Sophie

▷ Pierre, *mets-toi devant Maman (à côté de l'oncle Bernard, etc.)* .

1. Sylvie et Jacqueline, _____ .

2. Paul, _____ .

3. Catherine, _____ .

4. Charlotte, _____ .

A2. S'IL VOUS PLAÎT

Tell the following people not to do one thing, but to do the other. Follow the model, using the *imperative* form of the suggested reflexive verb.

▷ se mettre (ici / là-bas)

Annette, *ne te mets pas ici! Mets-toi là-bas!* _____

1. s'asseoir (sur la table / sur la chaise)

   Éric, _____

   _____

2. s'asseoir (à côté de Jacques / à côté de moi)

   Hélène et Martine, _____

   _____

3. s'acheter (des bandes dessinées / des livres intéressants)

   Pierre et Alain, _____

   _____

4. se laver (après le dîner / avant le dîner)

   Philippe, _____

   _____

B1. ALLÔ!

Read about the following people, and say which of the people mentioned in the box they are calling. Use the appropriate forms of **appeler.**

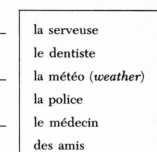

1. Tu vois un OVNI (*UFO*).

   _____

2. J'ai une mauvaise grippe (*flu*).

   _____

3. Nous voulons déjeuner.

   _____

4. Vous avez une carie (*cavity*).

   _____

5. Tu veux connaître le temps pour demain.

   _____

6. Mes cousins veulent organiser une boum.

   _____

la serveuse
le dentiste
la météo (*weather*)
la police
le médecin
des amis

C1. EXPRESSION PERSONNELLE

Say whether or not you do certain things with regularity. Use expressions with **tous / toutes** in *affirmative* or *negative* sentences. Follow the model.

▷ étudier / le jour?

Oui, j'étudie tous les jours. (Non, je n'étudie pas tous les jours.)

1. regarder la télé / le soir?

   _____

2. aller au cinéma / la semaine?

   _____

3. sortir / le samedi soir?

   _____

4. célébrer votre anniversaire / l'an?

   _____

TRADUCTION

Give the French equivalent of each of the following sentences.

1. *Be quiet, please!*

    _____

2. *Let's get ready for the party (la fête).*

    _____

3. *I work every day.*

    _____

4. *Everybody is here.*

    _____

POUR COMMUNIQUER La classe de français

Select six students from your French class, and say how they are seated in relation to you.

▷ *Thomas est à ma gauche.* _____

_____

_____

_____

_____

_____

UNITÉ 3   LE MARIAGE DE JACQUELINE
Leçon 3   Un garçon pressé

V1.A1.   DANS LA SALLE DE BAINS

The people below are in the bathroom, where they are using the objects illustrated. Say what they are doing, using the appropriate *reflexive* verbs.

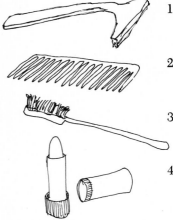

1. Mon père _se rase_____ .

   Jacques et Alain _____ .

2. Nous _____ .

   Tu _____ .

3. Vous _____ les dents.

   Je _____ les dents aussi.

4. Ma sœur _____ .

   Francine et Lucie _____ .

V2.A2.   OUI OU NON?

Read about the following people, and say whether or not they are doing the activities in parentheses.

1. Tu as une mauvaise grippe (*flu*). (se lever?)

   _____

2. J'entends du bruit (*noise*) dans la chambre. (se réveiller?)

   _____

3. Ma cousine va danser dans une discothèque très élégante. (se maquiller?)

   _____

4. Nous allons réparer (*to fix*) la voiture. (s'habiller bien?)

   _____

5. Je suis fatigué. (se coucher?)

   _____

6. François va mettre son pyjama. (se déshabiller avant?)

   _____

7. Nous avons joué au football. (se laver?)

   _____

8. Mes cousines vont nager. (se maquiller?)

   _____

V3.B1. COMMENT?

Say how we do certain things. Complete the sentences with the appropriate parts of the body.

▷ **On mange avec** *la bouche* _____ .

1. On entend avec _____ .
2. On fait du jogging avec _____ .
3. On regarde avec _____ .
4. On prend un stylo avec _____ .
5. On joue du piano avec _____ .
6. On respire (*breathes*) avec _____ .
7. On peut nager sur _____ ou sur _____ .
8. On joue au football européen (*soccer*) avec _____ .

B2. HYGIÈNE PERSONNELLE

Read about the following people, and say which parts of the body they are likely to wash.

▷ **Paul va déjeuner.** *Il se lave les mains.* _____

1. Annette a acheté du shampooing. _____
2. J'ai écrit avec un stylo qui fuit (*leaks*). _____
3. Vous allez chez le dentiste. _____
4. J'ai mis des sandales pour aller à la plage. _____

TRADUCTION

Give the French equivalent of each of the following sentences.

1. *We are getting up early tomorrow.* _____
2. *What time do you go to bed?* _____
3. *I am washing my hands.* _____
4. *My sister is brushing her hair.* _____

POUR COMMUNIQUER Le week-end

Write a short paragraph in which you tell at what time each member of your family, including yourself, gets up and goes to bed on weekends.

_____
_____
_____
_____
_____

UNITÉ 3   LE MARIAGE DE JACQUELINE
Leçon 4   La panne

A1.   JOYEUX ANNIVERSAIRE! (*Happy birthday!*)

The people below are celebrating their birthdays. Read the descriptions, and then say which of the following gifts they are receiving. Use the appropriate *present tense* forms of **recevoir**.

un livre / des disques / des boucles d'oreille / un appareil-photo / un vélo / un chien

1.   Nathalie est une fille très élégante.

_____

2.   Mes cousins aiment la musique.

_____

3.   Tu es un photographe amateur.

_____

4.   Nous aimons les animaux.

_____

5.   Vous aimez faire des promenades à la campagne.

_____

6.   J'aime lire.

_____

B1.   SUJETS D'INTÉRÊT

From what the people below are doing, it is easy to tell what their interests are. Express these interests, using the appropriate form of **s'intéresser à** and an item from the box. (Remember the contractions: **à + le → au, à + les → aux**.)

1.   Ma sœur lit «Mademoiselle».

_____

2.   Nous admirons John McEnroe.

_____

3.   Mes cousins vont au concert.

_____

4.   Je lis les critiques de films.

_____

5.   Vous travaillez pour votre candidat aux élections.

_____

6.   Tu visites les musées.

_____

la politique
le cinéma
l'art
la mode (*fashion*)
le tennis
la musique

B2.C1.   RÉACTIONS

Read what is happening, and describe the reactions of the people below. Use the appropriate form of one of the following verbs:

> s'amuser / s'arrêter / se dépêcher / s'impatienter / s'embêter / s'inquiéter /
> se mettre en colère / s'énerver

▷ **Mes amis ne sont pas à l'heure au rendez-vous.**

Je *m'énerve (m'inquiète)* .

1. Je rentre chez moi à trois heures du matin.

   Mes parents _____.

2. Je vois un feu rouge (*red light*).

   Je _____.

3. Votre cousin a eu un accident avec votre voiture.

   Vous _____.

4. L'examen commence dans dix minutes.

   Nous _____.

5. Ces étudiants américains sont à une boum où personne ne parle anglais.

   Ils _____.

6. Les élèves n'étudient pas.

   Le professeur _____.

7. Le film est excellent.

   Nous _____.

D1. **OUI OU NON?**

Read about the following people, and decide whether or not they are going to do the things in parentheses. Use the construction **aller** + *infinitive* of *reflexive* verbs in *affirmative* or *negative* sentences.

▷ **Nous sommes fiancés. (se marier?)**

Nous allons nous marier.

1. Paul et Nicole vont à une boum avec des amis sympathiques. (s'amuser? s'embêter?)

   _____

   _____

2. Tu es fatigué. (se promener? se reposer?)

   _____

   _____

3. Mon frère va au lit (*to bed*). (se raser? se coucher?)

   _____

   _____

4. Vous avez tort mais vous êtes poli(e) (*polite*). (s'excuser? se mettre en colère?)

   _____

   _____

5. Je suis un excellent élève. (s'énerver pendant la classe? se souvenir de la réponse?)

   _____

   _____

6. Mes cousins sont en retard pour leur rendez-vous (*appointment*) avec le professeur.
   (s'arrêter au café? se dépêcher?)

   _____

   _____

TRADUCTION

Give the French equivalent of each of the following sentences.

1. *I did not receive any letters today.*

_____

2. *When do you get angry?*

_____

3. *I am going to take a walk.*

_____

4. *Do you remember this boy?*

_____

POUR COMMUNIQUER   Vos sentiments (*Your feelings*)

Different occasions produce different moods in us. Describe the circumstances that give rise to the following feelings, by completing the sentences below.

1. Je m'amuse quand _____

_____ .

2. Je m'embête quand _____

_____ .

3. Je m'impatiente quand _____

_____ .

4. Je m'inquiète quand _____

_____ .

5. Je me mets en colère quand _____

_____ .

UNITÉ 3   LE MARIAGE DE JACQUELINE
Leçon 5   Une page de journal

A1.   QUERELLES (*Quarrels*)

The following people had arguments and don't speak to each other anymore. Answer the following questions. (Remember: **ne . . . plus** means *no . . . longer.*)

▷ **Pierre invite Bernard?**   *Non, ils ne s'invitent plus.*

▷ **Tu parles à Jacques?**   *Non, nous ne nous parlons plus.*

1.   Tu invites Françoise?   _____

2.   Charles téléphone à Suzanne?   _____

3.   André écrit à Francine?   _____

4.   Tu dis bonjour à Antoine?   _____

5.   Jacques aime Sophie?   _____

6.   Roméo voit Juliette?   _____

B1.   LE WEEK-END DERNIER

Read about what the following people did last weekend. Then say whether or not they had fun. Use the **passé composé** of **s'amuser** in *affirmative* or *negative* sentences.

▷ **Ma cousine a eu un accident.**   *Elle ne s'est pas amusée.*

1.   Vous êtes sortis avec des amis sympathiques.

_____

2.   Nous avons préparé l'examen de lundi.

_____

3.   Antoine et Henri sont allés à une boum.

_____

4.   Mélanie et Yvette sont sorties avec des garçons stupides.

_____

5.   J'ai travaillé.

_____

6.   Tu as vu un film de Woody Allen.

_____

7.   Pierre est allé danser.

_____

8.   Alice a été malade.

_____

B2. QU'EST-CE QU'ILS ONT FAIT?

Say where the people below went and what they did there. Choose a place from column A and an activity from column B. Study the model carefully. Be logical in your sentences.

A	**B**
à la campagne	à une conférence stupide	s'amuser	se maquiller
à la plage	à un rendez-vous (*date*,	s'embêter	se promener
dans la salle de bains	*appointment*) important	se regarder	se dépêcher
à la maison	à une boum	se raser	se reposer
devant la glace		se laver	

▷ Isabelle *est allée dans la salle de bains. Elle s'est maquillée.*

1. Paul et André _____

2. Charlotte et Sylvie _____

3. Je _____

4. Tu _____

5. Nous _____

6. Monsieur Bernard _____

7. Vous _____

8. Mes amies _____

TRADUCTION

Give the French equivalent of each of the following sentences.

1. *Paul and Marie often write each other.*

   _____

2. *We do not speak to one another.*

   _____

3. *Yesterday I woke up at eight.*

   _____

4. *Michèle and Monique did not have fun last night.*

   _____

POUR COMMUNIQUER Hier

Describe what you did yesterday. Use at least six reflexive verbs in the **passé composé**.

_____

_____

_____

_____

Récréation culturelle

Faire-part

Quand un jeune homme et une jeune fille décident de se fiancer ou de se marier, leurs familles annoncent cet heureux événement. Cette annonce s'appelle un «faire-part».

> **fiançailles**
>
> ---
>
> **Le docteur et Mme**
> **François VELTER**
> **M. et Mme André**
> **GAULUPEAU**
> sont heureux de faire part des
> fiançailles de leurs enfants
> **Béatrice et Pierre-Michel**
> **88100 Saint-Dié.**
> **69290 Grézieu-la-Varenne.**

Ce faire-part de fiançailles a été publié dans un journal français. Lisez-le attentivement (*carefully*).

1. Comment s'appelle le fiancé? _____

   Comment s'appelle la fiancée? _____

GLOSSAIRE: **fiançailles** *engagement*

Lisez attentivement le faire-part suivant.

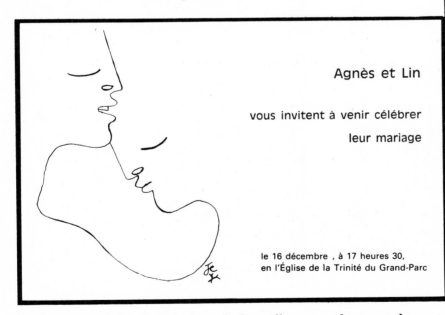

Agnès et Lin

vous invitent à venir célébrer

leur mariage

le 16 décembre , à 17 heures 30,
en l'Église de la Trinité du Grand-Parc

Madame Jacques DURIEZ,
Madame Henri FROMAGET,
Le Docteur et Madame Jean-Claude DURIEZ

ont la joie de vous faire part du mariage d'Agnès
avec Lin DAUBECH.

36, Rue Sainte-Croix de la Bretonnerie - Paris 4
14, Cours de Verdun - Bordeaux

Madame André LESCA,
Monsieur et Madame Georges DAUBECH

ont la joie de vous faire part du mariage de Lin
avec Agnès DURIEZ

17, Rue de Hourtins - Bordeaux
36, Avenue de Miremont - Bordeaux-Cauderan

3. Est-ce que c'est un faire-part de fiançailles ou un faire-part de mariage? _____

4. Comment s'appelle le jeune homme? _____

5. Comment s'appellent ses parents? _____

6. Comment s'appelle la jeune fille? _____

7. Est-ce que le mariage est un mariage civil ou un mariage religieux? _____

8. Quand et où a eu lieu le mariage? _____

_____

Unité 3

Récréation culturelle

Comment trouver l'ami(e) idéal(e)?

Il n'est pas toujours facile de trouver l'ami(e) idéal(e). **DATELINE FRANCE** propose de vous aider grâce à (*thanks to*) l'ordinateur (*computer*).

Dans le questionnaire suivant, on vous demande d'analyser votre personnalité. Remplissez (*Fill out*) ce questionnaire.

DATELINE: L'ORDINATEUR QUI FAIT LE BONHEUR.
REMPLISSEZ CE QUESTIONNAIRE.

M. ☐ Mme ☐ Mlle ☐

Nom ☐☐☐☐☐☐☐☐☐☐☐☐☐☐

Prénom ☐☐☐☐☐☐☐☐☐☐☐☐☐

N° et Rue ☐☐☐☐☐☐☐☐☐☐☐☐☐

Code Postal ☐☐☐☐☐

Ville ☐☐☐☐☐☐☐☐☐☐☐☐☐

Age ☐☐   Poids ☐☐   Taille ☐☐☐

Couleur de cheveux ☐☐☐☐☐☐☐☐☐

Profession ☐☐☐☐☐☐☐☐☐☐☐☐

Mes photos préférées sont : ☐ ☐ ☐

Je suis plutôt
Exubérant (e) ..... ☐
Intellectuel (le) .... ☐
Simple .... ☐
Volontaire .... ☐
Conciliant(e) ..... ☐
Rêveur (se) .... ☐
Actif (ve)........ ☐
Drôle .... ☐
Sérieux (se)...... ☐
Réservé (e) ...... ☐

J'aime
Parler .... ☐
Ecouter .... ☐
Ne rien faire ..... ☐
Voyager......... ☐
Faire du sport .... ☐
La pop music..... ☐
Le cinéma .... ☐
La lecture .... ☐
La mode .... ☐
L'argent......... ☐

Retourner ce questionnaire rempli à :
DATELINE FRANCE
15, avenue Victor Hugo - 75116 PARIS

GLOSSAIRE: **poids** *weight* **taille** *height* **plutôt** *rather* **exubérant** *full of life* **volontaire** *strong-willed* **conciliant** *conciliatory, willing to make peace* **rêveur** *dreamer* **lecture** *reading* **mode** *fashion*

Maintenant faites le portrait de l'époux (*husband*) idéal ou l'épouse (*wife*) idéale.

description physique: _____

qualités personnelles: _____

situation professionnelle: _____

autres caractéristiques: _____

Récréation culturelle

La solitude

Il y a des moments où nous avons l'impression d'être seul (*alone*) dans l'existence (*life*). Ce sentiment (*feeling*) s'appelle la solitude.

1. Est-ce qu'il y a des moments où vous éprouvez (*feel, expe-rience*) de la solitude? _____

    Qu'est-ce que vous faites dans ces situations? _____

    _____

    _____

2. Est-ce qu'il y a des moments où vous recherchez (*seek*)

    la solitude? _____

    Quand? Pourquoi? _____

    _____

    _____

Aujourd'hui, beaucoup de jeunes veulent «se trouver».

3. Qu'est-ce que vous faites pour vous trouver? _____

    _____

    _____

    _____

    _____

    _____

    _____

GLOSSAIRE: **vaincre** *to fight, overcome*   **le nôtre** *ours*   **rencontre** *meeting*
début *beginning*   **raison de vivre** *reason for living*   **fin** *end*

UNITÉ 4: *Accident*

INTRODUCTION: What you will do and learn in *Unité 4*

LESSON OPENERS

Hélène is furious because Henri failed to show up for a date. But Henri had a very valid excuse . . .

NOTES CULTURELLES

You will learn about teenage dating, about what young French people like to read, and about the mountain chain that separates France and Spain: *les Pyrénées.*

ACTIVITÉS

You will mainly practice a new way to talk about
past events, especially how   *pages in your textbook*

to describe what you used to do on a regular basis 215–216
to describe what you were doing at a certain point in time ... 217
to describe the circumstances that surrounded a particular
    event 221–222

You will also practice how

to talk about certain weather conditions 202
to express how long ago a certain event took place 204
to describe the furniture in your house 214
to tell for how long you have been doing certain things 227–228

STRUCTURE

You will learn a new past tense, the *imparfait* (imperfect), and when to use it instead of the *passé composé.* You will also learn a new verb: *rire* (to laugh).

UNITÉ 4 ACCIDENT
Leçon 1 Un rendez-vous manqué

VI. **LA MÉTÉO** (*The weather report*)

What we do or do not do often depends on the weather. From the information below, describe the weather. Use the appropriate weather expressions in the *present tense* (odd-numbered sentences) and the **passé composé** (even-numbered sentences).

▷ **Je ne sors pas.** *Il pleut. (Il neige, etc.)* _____

1. Vous faites du ski. _____
2. Je suis allé à la plage samedi. _____
3. Tu mets ton imperméable (*raincoat*). _____
4. Vous avez fait de la voile. _____
5. Isabelle porte des lunettes de soleil. _____
6. Nous sommes restés chez nous. _____
7. Oh là là, mon chapeau s'envole (*is flying away*). _____
8. Cet hiver, mes cousins ont fait du ski dans les Alpes. _____

A1. **VIVE LA DIFFÉRENCE!**

We all do things differently. Read what Pierre tells his cousins, and write what they answer. Use the **nous** form of the verbs in italics.

Pierre:

▷ **Je *nage* à la piscine.**

les cousins de Pierre:

Nous nageons à la plage.

1. Je *voyage* en juin. _____ en septembre.
2. Je *commence* mon travail (*job*) demain. _____ la semaine prochaine.
3. J'*envoie* une lettre à Brigitte. _____ une carte à Suzanne.
4. Je *paie* avec des traveller-chèques. _____ avec une carte de crédit.
5. J'*essaie* de parler français. _____ de parler espagnol.
6. Je *mange* dans un restaurant chinois. _____ dans un restaurant italien.

B1. QUAND?

Read what time or date it is. Then read when the people below did certain things. Say how long ago that was, using the word in parentheses in a construction with **il y a.** Look at the model.

▷ **Il est midi. Paul a téléphoné à huit heures ce matin. (heures)**

Il *a téléphoné il y a quatre heures* .

1. Il est trois heures vingt. Sylvie est sortie à trois heures. (minutes)

   Elle _____ .

2. Nous sommes vendredi. Mes cousins sont venus lundi. (jours)

   Ils _____ .

3. Nous sommes le 30 décembre. Isabelle est partie en France le 2 décembre. (semaines)

   Elle _____ .

4. Nous sommes en novembre. Janine s'est mariée en juillet. (mois)

   Elle _____ .

B2. EXPRESSION PERSONNELLE

Say when was the last time you did the following things. Use the construction **il y a** + elapsed time.

▷ **aller au cinéma?**

Je suis allé(e) au cinéma il y a une semaine.

1. dîner au restaurant?

   _____

2. aller à la piscine?

   _____

3. voir mes cousins?

   _____

4. recevoir une lettre?

   _____

V2. UNE INTERVIEW

Imagine that you are working for a French company that takes opinion polls. You want to learn about the habits of French students. Complete the questionnaire by filling in the blanks with **fois, temps,** or **heure**(s), as appropriate.

1. À quelle _____ est-ce que vous vous levez le matin?

2. Combien d'_____ étudiez-vous par *(per)* jour?

3. Combien de _____ par mois allez-vous au cinéma?

4. Le week-end, est-ce que vous avez le _____ d'étudier?

5. Quand vous avez un rendez-vous, êtes-vous généralement à l'_____ ?

6. Combien de _____ êtes-vous allé au concert cette année?

TRADUCTION

Give the French equivalent of each of the following sentences.

1. *It snowed yesterday and now it's raining.*

    _____

2. *This week I went to the movies three times.*

    _____

3. *Charles called two hours ago.*

    _____

4. *My parents bought their car five years ago.*

    _____

POUR COMMUNIQUER L'année dernière

Describe five or six important things you did last year, and say how long ago you did them. Use the construction **il y a** + elapsed time.

_____

_____

_____

_____

_____

_____

_____

UNITÉ 4 ACCIDENT
Leçon 2 Mauvaise humeur

A1. À L'ÉTRANGER (*Abroad*)

The people below spent some time in the cities mentioned in parentheses. Say which of the following languages they spoke there. Use the *imperfect* of **parler.**

français / anglais / espagnol / allemand

⇨ (à Genève) Philippe *parlait français* .

1. (à Munich) Mes parents _____ .
2. (à Paris) Je _____ .
3. (à Londres) Nous _____ .
4. (à San Francisco) Tu _____ .
5. (à Québec) Tu _____ .
6. (à Buenos Aires) Vous _____ .
7. (à Vienne) Sylvie _____ .
8. (à San Juan) Thomas et André _____ .

A2. VIVE LES VACANCES!

For French teenagers, vacation is a time for relaxation and not for working. Complete the first sentence of each item with the *negative* form of the *imperfect* of **travailler.** In the second sentence, describe the person's vacation activities by using the *imperfect* of the verb suggested by the drawing.

⇨ Pendant les vacances, Thérèse *ne travaillait pas* .
Généralement, elle *jouait au tennis* .

1. André et Jean _____ .
Généralement, _____ .

2. Vous _____ .
Généralement, _____ .

3. Je _____ .
Généralement, _____ .

4. Tu _____ .
Généralement, _____ .

5. Marc _____ .
Généralement, _____ .

6. Nous _____ .
Généralement, _____ .

A3. TOUT CHANGE (*Everything changes*)

Say whether or not you used to do the following things *five* years ago. Use the *imperfect tense* in *affirmative* or *negative* sentences.

▷ habiter dans cette ville?

Il y a cinq ans, j'habitais (je n'habitais pas) dans cette ville.

1. aller à cette école?

   _____

2. aller souvent au cinéma?

   _____

3. apprendre le français?

   _____

4. avoir un appareil-photo?

   _____

5. avoir mes amis d'aujourd'hui?

   _____

6. organiser des boums?

   _____

7. sortir beaucoup?

   _____

8. faire du camping?

   _____

A4. LES ENFANTS MODÈLES (*Perfect children*)

When they were young, the following people were perfect children. Say whether or not they used to do the things in parentheses. Use the *imperfect tense*.

1. Jacques (aider sa mère? faire les courses? obéir à son père?)

   _____

   _____

2. Suzanne et Hélène (lire beaucoup? perdre leur temps? s'énerver?)

   _____

   _____

3. nous (avoir beaucoup d'amis? faire des tours [*tricks*] à nos amis? nous mettre en colère?)

   _____

   _____

4. vous (critiquer vos amis? dire des mensonges?)

   _____

   _____

5. je (étudier? réussir à mes examens? m'embêter en classe?)

   _____

   _____

6. tu (rendre visite à tes grands-parents? attendre tes amis? t'impatienter?)

   _____

   _____

B1. OÙ ÉTAIENT-ILS?

Read what the following people did Saturday afternoon. Then say whether or not they were at home. Use the construction **être chez** + stress pronoun in *affirmative* or *negative* sentences.

▷ **Georges a nagé.**   *Il n'était pas chez lui.* _____

1. Gisèle a fait les courses.   _____

2. Nous avons fait la cuisine.   _____

3. Tu as joué au tennis.   _____

4. Je suis allé au cinéma.   _____

5. Vous vous êtes promenés.   _____

6. Albert a lu un livre.   _____

7. Les élèves ont étudié.   _____

8. Charles est sorti avec sa fiancée.   _____

TRADUCTION

Give the French equivalent of each of the following sentences.

1. *What's wrong?*

    _____

2. *What happened yesterday?*

    _____

3. *—You were home yesterday? —Yes, I was home!*

    _____

4. *—Paul was not with Suzanne? —Yes, he was with her!*

    _____

POUR COMMUNIQUER   Hier soir

Ask four friends where they were last night at nine o'clock and what they were doing there. Then write about what they told you.

_____

_____

_____

_____

_____

_____

_____

UNITÉ 4 ACCIDENT
Leçon 3 À l'hôpital

V1. **CHAQUE CHOSE À SA PLACE!** (*Everything in its place!*)

Sylvie tells her little brother Éric what to do. Complete her sentences with the appropriate *appliance* or piece of *furniture*.

➜ **Mets le lait dans** *le réfrigérateur* .

1. Ces assiettes (*plates*) sont sales (*dirty*). Mets-les dans _____ .

2. Ces assiettes sont propres (*clean*). Mets-les dans _____ .

3. Ces chemises sont sales. Mets-les dans _____ .

4. Ces chemises sont propres. Mets-les dans _____ .

5. Tu veux écrire une lettre? Utilise _____ .

6. Prends ce livre et mets-le dans _____ .

7. Tu veux décorer ta chambre? Mets des _____ ou

   des _____ sur le mur (*wall*).

8. Tu es fatigué! Assieds-toi sur _____ ou sur _____ .

9. Tu veux dormir? Repose-toi sur _____ .

A1. **C'ÉTAIT LA BELLE VIE!** (*The great life!*)

When Jacques was in France last summer he wrote to his sister Lise in Québec, giving her the details about his daily life. Now he is remembering what he used to do during his stay in France. Write out his thoughts, using the *imperfect*.

la lettre:

Ma Chère Lise,

Je fais beaucoup de choses. Le matin, je me promène ou je joue au tennis. L'après-midi, je vais à la plage où je rencontre Sylvie, une fille qui est très sympathique. Nous nageons et nous jouons au volley. Ensuite, nous allons au café où nous rencontrons nos amis. Ils sont intelligents et leur conversation est intéressante. Je dîne généralement à huit heures. Après, je sors avec Sylvie. Nous allons dans une discothèque où nous dansons jusqu'à une heure du matin. Je pense que je suis amoureux d'elle.

C'est la belle vie! Jacques

les souvenirs (*memories*):

En France, je faisais beaucoup de choses.

_____

_____

_____

_____

_____

_____

_____

_____

_____

_____

_____

_____

_____

A2. LE 14 JUILLET

July fourteenth, or Bastille Day, is the French national holiday. It is always a special occasion. Say that on the evening of July 14, the following people did things that they were not used to doing during the rest of July. Study the model.

		d'habitude:	le 14 juillet:
⇨	(dîner)	Paul __*dînait*__ chez lui.	__*Il a dîné*__ au restaurant.
1.	(aller)	Hélène ____ au cinéma.	____ au concert.
2.	(boire)	Charles ____ de l'eau minérale.	____ du champagne.
3.	(regarder)	Nathalie ____ la télé.	____ les feux d'artifice (*fireworks*).
4.	(se coucher)	Éric ____ tôt.	____ très tard.
5.	(dormir)	Alain ____ huit heures.	____ seulement trois heures.

A3. SPORTS ET LOISIRS (*Leisure activities*)

During vacation, people have many different leisure activities. Describe the activities of the following people by filling in the blanks with the appropriate forms of the verb **jouer.** Use the *imperfect* for regular activities and the **passé composé** for occasional activities.

1. En général, je ____ au tennis.

2. Un jour, nous ____ au volleyball.

3. Le 10 juillet, Charles ____ au golf avec moi.

4. Le samedi après-midi, vous ____ au bridge.

5. D'habitude, avant le dîner tu ____ aux échecs (*chess*).

6. Une ou deux fois, Henri ____ au ping-pong avec nous.

7. Un week-end, Marc ____ au Monopoly.

A4. AVEZ-VOUS BONNE MÉMOIRE?

Say whether or not the people below used to do the things indicated in parentheses.

1. (parler français? travailler le week-end? se coucher tard?)

    Il y a un an, je __*(ne) parlais (pas) français. Je*__ ____

    ____

2. (habiter ici? avoir leur voiture? travailler beaucoup?)

    Il y a cinq ans, mes parents ____

    ____

3. (avoir beaucoup de petites voitures? consommer [*consume*] beaucoup d'énergie?)

    Il y a dix ans, les Américains ____

    ____

4. (utiliser des ordinateurs? voyager en avion? être très heureux?)

    En 1900, les gens ____

    ____

B1. LA PANNE (*The power failure*)

Look at the drawing, and say what the following people were doing at the time of the power failure yesterday.

> Charles *lisait un livre (regardait des bandes dessinées ...)*.

1. Les Durand _____.

2. Les Dupont _____.

3. M. Robert _____.

4. Mme Mercier _____.

5. M. Thomas _____.

6. Paul _____.

7. Hélène _____.

8. M. Imbert _____.

TRADUCTION

Give the French equivalent of each of the following sentences.

1. *Jacques broke his leg.*

   _____

2. *On Mondays we used to play tennis.*

   _____

3. *Usually I played well, but one day I lost.*

   _____

4. *What were you doing at nine o'clock?*

   _____

POUR COMMUNIQUER   Retour à la maison (*Return home*)

Write six sentences describing what different members of your family were doing and where they were when you came home yesterday. Describe either real or imagined activities.

_____

_____

_____

_____

_____

_____

_____

UNITÉ 4 ACCIDENT
Leçon 4 La visite du commissaire

A1. À QUEL ÂGE?

Say how old the following people were when they did the things indicated.

▷ (apprendre à parler) *J'avais deux ans quand j'ai appris à parler* .

1. (apprendre à lire)   J'_____ .
2. (apprendre à nager)   J'_____ .
3. (apprendre à conduire) Ma grande sœur _____

    _____ .

4. (se marier)   Mon père _____ .
5. (se marier)   Ma mère _____ .

A2. UN PIQUE-NIQUE

Describe the last picnic to which you went. Answer the questions below in complete sentences.

1. Quel jour était-ce? _____

2. Quel temps faisait-il? _____

3. Où était le pique-nique? _____

4. Combien d'invités est-ce qu'il y avait? Combien de garçons? Combien de filles? _____

    _____

5. Est-ce que vous connaissiez tout le monde? _____

6. Quels vêtements portiez-vous ce jour-là? _____

7. Qui a organisé le pique-nique? _____

8. Est-ce que vous avez apporté quelque chose au pique-nique? Quoi (*What*)? _____

    _____

9. Qu'est-ce que vous avez fait avant le pique-nique? _____

    _____

10. Qu'est-ce que vous avez mangé? _____

11. Qu'est-ce que vous avez bu? _____

12. Qu'est-ce que vous avez fait après le pique-nique? _____

    _____

A3. UN CAMBRIOLAGE (A burglary)

Imagine that you witnessed a burglary at the **Banque de France** and that you recorded your observations on the cassette player you were carrying. Now you are going over your recording and writing out a report for the police. Be sure to use the **passé composé** and the *imperfect*, as appropriate.
(Note: A main action is indicated by MA; the circumstances of this action are indicated by C.)

le texte de la cassette:

votre déclaration:

▷ **Il est 9 heures 10. (C)** *Il était neuf heures dix.* _____

1. Je rentre chez moi. (C) _____

2. Je vois un homme . . . (MA) _____

3. . . . qui vient de la rue Pasteur. (C) _____

4. Il est grand. (C) _____

5. Il porte un costume bleu. (C) _____

6. Il a une moustache. (C) _____

7. Il entre dans un café. (MA) _____

8. Il téléphone. (MA) _____

9. Il attend dix minutes. (MA) _____

10. Une voiture arrive. (MA) _____

11. C'est une voiture bleue. (C) _____

12. Dans cette voiture, il y a quatre personnes. (C) _____

13. L'homme sort du café. (MA) _____

14. Il monte dans la voiture. (MA) _____

15. Je note le numéro. (MA) _____

16. C'est le numéro 9181TTB75. (C) _____

A4.   UN ACCIDENT

Imagine that you have just witnessed the following accident. Describe what you saw, using the suggested verbs in affirmative or negative sentences.

Les circonstances de l'accident:

l'heure: _____ (être)

le temps: _____ (faire / neiger)

le jeune homme: _____ (porter / conduire / aller)

_____

_____

L'accident:

le chien: _____ (traverser: *to cross*)

le jeune homme: _____ (faire attention / voir /
_____ déraper / tomber /
_____ se casser la jambe)

B1.   SOUVENIRS PERSONNELS (*Memories*)

Complete the sentences below with expressions of your choice. If you describe a regular event, use the *imperfect*. If you describe an event which happened only once, use the **passé composé**.

▷   **Quand j'avais cinq ans,** *nous habitions à New York (je suis allé en Californie ...)* .

1.   Quand j'avais huit ans, _____ .

2.   Quand j'avais dix ans, _____ .

3.   Quand j'avais douze ans, _____ .

4.   En 1980, _____ .

5.   En 1984, _____ .

B2. POURQUOI?

Describe why the people below did certain things. Use elements of columns A and B in logical sentences. Use the *imperfect* and the **passé composé,** as appropriate.

A		B	
étudier	insister	avoir faim	avoir tort
mettre un pull	se dépêcher	avoir soif	avoir raison
aller au restaurant	s'excuser	avoir froid	avoir un examen
boire du Coca-Cola	acheter du pain	avoir chaud	avoir un rendez-vous
rester à la maison	s'arrêter dans un café		

▷ Philippe *s'est excusé parce qu'il avait tort* _____ .

1. Nous _____ .

2. Vous _____ .

3. Tu _____ .

4. Richard _____ .

5. Mes cousins _____ .

6. Pierre et Henri _____ .

7. Je _____ .

8. Mes amies _____ .

TRADUCTION

Give the French equivalent of each of the following sentences.

1. *I didn't see the (license) number of the car.*

_____

2. *When Pierre arrived, it was three o'clock.*

_____

3. *I stayed home because I was sick.*

_____

4. *Sylvie was reading when Paul phoned her.*

_____

POUR COMMUNIQUER   Un événement

Describe an event in your life. It may be a happy event (a party, a wedding, a graduation) or a sad event (an accident, etc.). Describe when the event occurred, how old you were, how you were feeling, what happened, who did what . . .

_____

_____

_____

_____

_____

UNITÉ 4   ACCIDENT
Leçon 5   Réconciliation

A1.   RIRES

Can you tell whether the following people are laughing or not? Read each sentence carefully and then write out what you think, using the verb **rire**. The verbs in both sentences should be in the same tense.

▷   **Paul voit un film drôle.**   *Il rit.* _____

▷   **Je suis tombé dans la rue.**   *Je n'ai pas ri.* _____

1.   Nous lisons un livre amusant. _____

2.   Vous avez écouté quelque chose de drôle. _____

3.   Paul se coupe. _____

4.   Jacques et Pierre n'ont pas réussi
     à leurs examens. _____

5.   Hélène a eu un accident. _____

6.   Je regarde une pièce comique. _____

7.   Nous voyons une comédie amusante. _____

8.   J'écoutais un bon comédien. _____

9.   Mes amis étaient de bonne humeur. _____

10.   Tu étais de mauvaise humeur. _____

B1.   LE RECENSEMENT (*Census*)

An employee from the French Census Bureau wants to know how long certain people have been living in this city. Give him the information by counting the number of years between the date when the following people moved here and the present.

▷   **M. Lambert: 1960**   *M. Lambert habite ici depuis 29 (30...) ans.*

1.   mes cousins: 1980 _____

2.   nous: 1975 _____

3.   vous: 1983 _____

4.   toi: 1970 _____

5.   moi: 1978 _____

6.   mon grand-père: 1945 _____

B2.   UN QUESTIONNAIRE

Imagine that a French journalist is writing an article about young American people. He is asking you the following questions about your own activities. Answer him affirmatively, saying for *how long* you have been doing these things. Use your imagination, if necessary.

▷   **Vous apprenez le français?**   *Oui, j'apprends le français depuis deux ans (18 ans, 1982, ...).*

1.   Vous jouez au tennis? _____

2.   Vous savez nager? _____

3. Vous faites du jogging? _____

4. Vous habitez dans cette ville? _____

5. Vous allez à cette école? _____

6. Vous avez un vélo? _____

B3. DEPUIS QUAND?

Read when people arrived at a certain place. Then read about the present time or date. Say for *how long* the people have done the activity suggested in parentheses, using the verb and the expression in parentheses.

▷ **Paul est arrivé à la piscine à 2 heures. Il est 2 heures 30.** (nager / minutes)

Il nage depuis 30 minutes. _____

1. Nous sommes arrivés sur le court de tennis à 3 heures. Il est 5 heures. (jouer au tennis / heures)

_____

2. Mon cousin est arrivé à Paris en juin. Nous sommes en décembre. (habiter à Paris / mois)

_____

3. Janine est arrivée dans cet hôpital le 3 octobre. Nous sommes le 23 octobre.
(travailler dans cet hôpital / jours)

_____

4. Je suis arrivé à la bibliothèque à 5 heures moins le quart. Il est 5 heures 20. (étudier / minutes)

_____

TRADUCTION

Give the French equivalent of each of the following sentences.

1. *My little brother cried when he went to the dentist.*

_____

2. *Thérèse has been at the hospital since Sunday.*

_____

3. *We have been waiting for two hours.*

_____

4. *For how long have you been here?*

_____

POUR COMMUNIQUER   Votre copain français

You are writing to François, your French friend. In the letter, tell him about five things that you have been doing for a certain time and ask him related questions.

▷ *J'apprends le français depuis deux ans. Depuis combien de temps apprends-tu l'anglais?*

_____

_____

Récréation culturelle

La presse francophone

La presse francophone comprend (*includes*) non seulement les magazines et journaux français mais aussi tous les magazines et journaux de langue (*language*) française publiés dans le monde (*world*). Regardez bien les magazines.

1. Comment s'appelle ce magazine?

   _____

2. Quel événement est décrit dans ce magazine?

   _____

3. En quelle année (*year*) est-ce qu'il a eu lieu?

   _____

4. De quelle nationalité est le couple princier?

   _____

Ce magazine donne les progrâmmes de télévision de chaque semaine.

5. Comment s'appelle ce magazine?

   _____

Sur la couverture (*cover*), il y a une photo d'un acteur américain très populaire en France.

6. Qui est cet acteur? _____

   _____

7. Avez-vous vu des films avec cet acteur?

   _____

   Quels films? _____

   _____

Unité 4

Récréation culturelle

Tintin

LE SECRET de LA LICORNE

HERGÉ

© by Editions Casterman, Paris.

GLOSSAIRE: **licorne** *unicorn* **Je ne me trompe pas** *I'm not mistaken* **À la recherche d'occasions?** *Looking for second-hand bargains?* **empêcher** *to prevent* **découvrir** *to discover* **marchander** *to bargain* **voler** *to steal* **portefeuille** *wallet* **Tu l'auras . . . oublié** *You probably forgot it* **tiens** *hold* **moi-même** *myself* **Ça n'arrive jamais qu'à toi** *That only happens to you* **des histoires pareilles** *those kinds of things* **Se laisser . . . voler** *To let someone steal* **le mien** *mine*

Récréation culturelle

Les «Aventures de Tintin» ont un très grand succès en France et dans les pays d'expression française (*French-speaking*). Elles ont été traduites en anglais, en allemand, en espagnol, en italien, en japonais et dans beaucoup d'autres langues. Tintin, le héros principal, est un jeune détective. Il est accompagné dans ses nombreuses expéditions par son chien Milou. Parmi (*Among*) les autres personnages, il y a Dupont et Dupond, deux policiers très naïfs. La page de gauche représente la première page de l'album Tintin intitulé «Le Secret de la Licorne».

1. Décrivez les personnages suivants:

   Tintin   _____

   _____

   _____

   Milou   _____

   _____

   _____

   Dupont et Dupond   _____

   _____

   _____

2. En un paragraphe de dix lignes, décrivez les événements qui sont illustrés sur la page de gauche.

   _____

   _____

   _____

   _____

   _____

   _____

   _____

   _____

   _____

UNITÉ 5: *Madame R*

INTRODUCTION: What you will do and learn in *Unité 5*

LESSON OPENERS

Madame R, a famous fortuneteller, sees a very exciting vacation in store for Sophie. Christine, Sophie's friend, remains unconvinced. Will Madame R's predictions come true?

NOTES CULTURELLES

You will learn about how and where young French people spend their vacations. You will learn about two French-speaking islands: Corsica and Tahiti. And you will learn about an important event in French towns and villages: *la fête foraine* (the carnival).

ACTIVITÉS

You will practice how   *pages in your textbook*

STRUCTURE

You will learn mainly about the future tense, which is used to talk about future events. You will be introduced to the conditional tense. You will learn the forms and uses of interrogative pronouns. And you will learn two new verbs: *vivre* (to live) and *croire* (to believe).

UNITÉ 5   MADAME R
Leçon 1   La fête foraine

A1.   PLUS OU MOINS?

Compare the following by using the *comparative* form of the suggested adjectives.

▷   **une moto / rapide / une auto**
Une moto est plus (moins, aussi) rapide qu'une auto.

1.   le français / facile / l'espagnol

_____

2.   l'hydrogène / lourd / l'air

_____

3.   une Mercédès / chère / une Renault

_____

4.   l'amitié / durable (*lasting*) / l'amour

_____

5.   le Coca-Cola / bon / l'eau minérale

_____

6.   la planche à voile / dangereuse / le ski

_____

A2.   COMPARAISONS PERSONNELLES

Compare the following people in two sentences. Choose appropriate adjectives. (You may wish to consult the **Vocabulaires pratiques** on pages 17, 142, and 236 of your textbook.)

▷   **moi / mon meilleur ami** *Je suis moins âgé(e) que mon meilleur ami. Je suis plus grand(e) que lui.*
1.   moi / ma meilleure amie _____
2.   les Américains / les Français _____
3.   les hommes / les femmes _____
4.   les gens d'aujourd'hui / les gens d'autrefois _____

B1.   LOGIQUE!

Read the following comparisons. Then compare the people again, using the verb **avoir** and the nouns in parentheses. Be logical!

▷   **Nathalie est plus riche que Pierre. (l'argent)**
Elle a plus d'argent que lui.

1.   François est moins intelligent que sa sœur. (les idées)

_____

2.   Joseph est plus heureux que ses cousins. (les problèmes)

_____

3. Monique est plus égoïste que son frère. (les amis)

_____

4. Philippe est aussi riche que Georges. (l'argent)

_____

5. Vous êtes aussi patients que Louis. (la patience)

_____

C1.   À VOTRE AVIS (*In your opinion*)

According to you, which are the people or things that are the best in the following categories? Use the *superlative* construction to express your choices.

▷   **un magazine intéressant**   *Le magazine le plus intéressant est "Time Magazine" ("Sports Illustrated"...).*

1. une voiture rapide?   _____
2. une voiture chère?   _____
3. des sports intéressants?   _____
4. une belle ville?   _____
5. un bon orchestre?   _____
6. des bons acteurs?   _____
7. une bonne équipe (*team*) de baseball?   _____

TRADUCTION

Give the French equivalent of each of the following sentences.

1. *Don't waste your money!* _____
2. *My brother is older than I, but I am more intelligent than he.* _____

_____

3. *Do you have more money than Anne?* _____
4. *Stéphanie is the nicest girl in the class.* _____

_____

POUR COMMUNIQUER   Comparaisons

Compare yourself to one of your friends or to a TV personality. Write six or seven sentences.

_____

_____

_____

_____

UNITÉ 5   MADAME R

Leçon 2   Les prédictions de Madame R

A1.   WEEK-END

Read about the following people, and say who will stay home and who will go out. Use the *future* forms of **rester à la maison** or **sortir,** as appropriate.

1.   Paul est malade.   _____

2.   Je dois étudier.   _____

3.   Nous devons faire les courses.   _____

4.   Je veux aller au cinéma.   _____

5.   Caroline a un rendez-vous.   _____

6.   Hélène et Sylvie vont aller danser.   _____

7.   Les élèves doivent préparer l'examen.   _____

8.   Tu vas jouer au football.   _____

A2.   PROJETS DE VOYAGE

In planning her trip to France, Michèle wrote the following notes. Now she tells her mother about her plans, and later her mother tells a friend about them. Write what Michèle and her mother say.

Notes: arriver à Paris le 10 juillet / rester là une semaine / visiter Notre-Dame / monter à la tour Eiffel / sortir avec Béatrice / partir de Paris le 17 juillet / prendre le train / visiter la Provence / rentrer en Amérique le 1er août

Michèle:

J'arriverai à Paris le 10 juillet.
Je resterai là _____

_____

_____

_____

_____

_____

_____

la mère de Michèle:

Michèle arrivera à Paris

_____

_____

_____

_____

_____

_____

_____

A3. L'ORDRE CHRONOLOGIQUE

We do most things in a certain sequence. Say what the following people will do, using a logical sequence.

▷ (prendre l'avion / acheter son billet)

Paul *achètera son billet. Ensuite, il prendra l'avion.*

1. (dîner / se laver les mains)

   Jacques _____

2. (dormir / se coucher)

   Nous _____

3. (célébrer la victoire / gagner)

   Vous _____

4. (prendre ton passeport / partir en voyage)

   Tu _____

5. (acheter une moto / gagner de l'argent)

   Je _____

6. (se marier / tomber amoureux)

   Pierre et Catherine _____

B1. NON!

Read about the following people, and say that they will *not* do one of the activities in the box. Use the *future* in *negative* sentences. Be logical.

1. Vous n'avez pas de passeport.

   _____

2. Tu n'as pas sommeil.

   _____

3. Charles n'est pas poli (*polite*).

   _____

4. Je n'ai pas faim.

   _____

5. Nous sommes très patients.

   _____

6. Bernard est impatient.

   _____

7. Mes amis mangent beaucoup.

   _____

8. Vous êtes paresseux.

   _____

> attendre
> travailler
> déjeuner
> voyager
> maigrir
> dormir
> s'énerver
> s'excuser

B2. PRÉDICTIONS

Say whether or not the following people will do the things in parentheses within the next three years.

1. (gagner beaucoup d'argent? piloter un avion? acheter une moto?)

   Je _____

   _____

2. (se marier? acheter une moto? trouver un trésor [*treasure*]?)

   Mon meilleur ami _____

   _____

3. (acheter une très grande maison? visiter la Chine? vendre leur auto?)

   Mes parents _____

   _____

4. (manger des aliments [*food*] artificiels? passer les vacances sur la lune [*moon*]? utiliser des robots?)

   On _____

   _____

TRADUCTION

Give the French equivalent of each of the following sentences.

1. *I will buy my ticket tomorrow.*

   _____

2. *We will travel by car.*

   _____

3. *Pierre will not visit Paris with us.*

   _____

4. *When will you write to your parents?*

   _____

POUR COMMUNIQUER Un voyage en France

Imagine that you are the leader of a student bicycle tour of France. Plan the trip. You may use the following verbs:

voyager / arriver / rester / visiter / prendre / partir / rentrer

_____

_____

_____

_____

_____

_____

_____

UNITÉ 5 MADAME R

Leçon 3 Une île romantique

A1. CE SOIR

What we do often determines how we feel later on. Read about the following people, and say how they will feel tonight. Use the *future* of **être** and the correct form of one of the adjectives in the box.

maintenant: ce soir:

1. Nous jouons au football.   _____

    _____

2. Tu dors.   _____

    _____

3. Marc dit au revoir à sa fiancée. _____

    _____

4. Vous mangez trop.   _____

    _____

5. Je perds un match important. _____

    _____

6. Mes cousines sortent avec des garçons sympathiques. _____

furieux
fatigué
malade
triste
content
reposé

A2. L'ANNÉE PROCHAINE (*Next year*)

Say whether or not you will do any of the following things next year.

▷ faire du français?   *Oui, je ferai du français.*
                            (Non, je ne ferai pas de français.)

1. faire de l'espagnol?   _____

2. faire un grand voyage?   _____

3. aller en vacances?   _____

4. aller en Italie?   _____

5. avoir une auto?   _____

6. avoir plus d'argent qu'aujourd'hui? _____

7. être plus indépendant(e)?   _____

8. être plus heureux (heureuse)? _____

B1. QU'EST-CE QU'ILS FERONT?

Say what the people below will do under specific circumstances. Use elements of columns A and B in logical sentences.

A	B
être malade	se reposer
jouer bien	aller au café
avoir de l'argent	acheter une auto
étudier	faire des progrès
gagner à la loterie	gagner le match
avoir soif	faire un voyage
être fatigué	aller chez le médecin

▷ Si Hélène *est fatiguée, elle se reposera* _____ .

1. Si mes parents _____ .

2. Si nous _____ .

3. Si vous _____ .

4. Si tu _____ .

5. Si je _____ .

6. Si Jacques _____ .

B2. EXPRESSION PERSONNELLE

Complete the sentences below with an expression of your choice.

1. Si je travaille cet été, _____

    _____ .

2. Si je ne vais pas à l'université, _____

    _____ .

3. Si mes parents me prêtent la voiture ce week-end, _____

    _____ .

4. Si un jour je suis millionnaire, _____

    _____ .

C1. PLUS TARD!

There are many things we cannot do now, but that we will be able to do later. Express this according to the model.

▷ **Parce que je n'ai pas d'argent, je n'achète pas de disques.**

Quand j'aurai de l'argent, j'achèterai des disques.

1. Parce que Paul ne travaille pas, il ne gagne pas d'argent.

   _____

2. Parce qu'il ne fait pas beau, vous n'allez pas à la plage.

   _____

3. Parce que nous n'avons pas 18 ans, nous ne votons pas.

   _____

4. Parce que mes amis n'ont pas le permis (_driver's license_), ils ne conduisent pas.

   _____

5. Parce que je n'ai pas ton adresse, je ne t'écris pas.

   _____

C2. EXPRESSION PERSONNELLE

Complete the sentences below with an expression of your choice.

1. Quand je travaillerai, _____ .
2. Quand j'aurai 20 ans, _____ .
3. Quand j'aurai 30 ans, _____ .
4. Je serai totalement indépendant(e) quand _____ .
5. Je me marierai quand _____ .

TRADUCTION

Give the French equivalent of each of the following sentences.

1. _One day I will go to Paris._

   _____

2. _My father will not be happy if I do not study._

   _____

3. _When Éric will work, he will buy a car._

   _____

4. _Where will you live when you are 20 years old?_

   _____

POUR COMMUNIQUER Voyages

Imagine that you have enough money to go on a trip this summer. Say where you will go and what you will do there.

_____

_____

_____

_____

_____

_____

_____

_____

_____

_____

UNITÉ 5   MADAME R
Leçon 4   L'erreur de Madame R

A1.   DEMAIN!

Complete the following sentences with the appropriate *future* forms of the verbs in parentheses.

1. (venir)   Paul _____ chez moi. Est-ce que vous _____ avec lui?

2. (pouvoir)   Je _____ prendre la voiture de mon frère. Nous _____ aller à la plage.

3. (envoyer)   J'_____ une lettre à mes grands-parents. Ils m'_____ de l'argent.

4. (voir)   Antoine _____ Juliette. Ils _____ un film ensemble.

5. (recevoir) Vous _____ un «B» à l'examen. Moi, je _____ un «A»!

6. (devoir)   Mon père _____ travailler à la maison. Nous _____ l'aider.

7. (vouloir)   Pierre _____ t'inviter. Est-ce que tu _____ aller chez lui?

8. (savoir)   Je _____ la réponse de François. Nous _____ s'il peut vous prêter sa moto.

B1.   OÙ?

The following people are citizens of the countries in which they live. Match each person with the proper city, and complete the statements with the *present* form of **vivre**. Les villes: **Atlanta, Rome, Moscou, Paris, Québec, Mexico, Genève, Berlin, Lisbonne.**

▷ **Peter est allemand.**   Il *vit à Berlin* _____ .

1. Paul est suisse.   Il _____ .

2. Lise est canadienne.   Elle _____ .

3. Igor et Boris sont russes.   Ils _____ .

4. Nous sommes portugais.   Nous _____ .

5. Vous êtes français.   Vous _____ .

6. Je suis italien.   Je _____ .

7. Tu es américaine.   Tu _____ .

8. Luis et José sont mexicains.   Ils _____ .

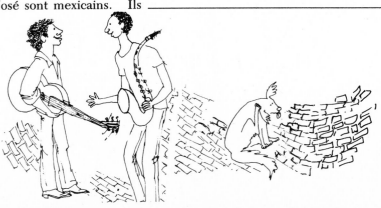

V1. EN QUELLE MATIÈRE?

Imagine that you are selling the various items mentioned below. Ask your customers which material they prefer. Complete the questions with a material that fits logically.

▷ Voulez-vous une robe *en laine (en coton, en nylon)* ?

1. Voulez-vous une chemise _____ ?
2. Voulez-vous un bracelet _____ ?
3. Voulez-vous un peigne _____ ?
4. Voulez-vous des boucles d'oreille _____ ?
5. Voulez-vous un vase _____ ?
6. Voulez-vous des casseroles (*pots*) _____ ?
7. Voulez-vous une chaise _____ ?
8. Voulez-vous une maison _____ ?

C1. DERRIÈRE LA PORTE

Little Éric is behind the door eavesdropping on a conversation between his brother Marc and some friends. He cannot hear Marc's first words. Fill them in.

Marc:		les amis de Marc:
▷ *À quoi* , pensez-vous?		À la boum!
1. _____, parles-tu?		De ma nouvelle moto.
2. _____, parles-tu?		De la petite amie de Robert.
3. _____, sors-tu?		Avec Sophie.
4. _____, t'intéresses-tu?		À la musique.
5. _____, as-tu besoin?		De vacances.
6. _____, as-tu envie?		D'une glace!
7. _____, écris-tu?		À Mireille.
8. _____, écrit-il?		Avec le crayon de Jacques.

D1. LA JOURNÉE DE PAUL

Brigitte asks Paul what he did today. From his answers, complete Brigitte's questions with **Qui est-ce que** or **Qu'est-ce que,** as appropriate.

Brigitte:	Paul:
1. _____ tu as rencontré?	Charles et Marie.
2. _____ tu as vu?	Jacques.
3. _____ tu as vu au cinéma?	Un western.
4. _____ tu as acheté?	Du pain.
5. _____ tu as invité?	Henri.
6. _____ tu as fait?	J'ai fait une promenade.

E1.   LE RETOUR DE MONSIEUR HULOT (*Mr. Hulot's return*)

Monsieur Hulot took a day off. When he came back to his office, he asked the secretary what happened. From the secretary's answers, complete Monsieur Hulot's questions with **Qui** or **Qu'est-ce qui**, as appropriate.

Monsieur Hulot: **la secrétaire:**

1. _____ a téléphoné?   Monsieur Durand.

2. _____ est arrivé?   Une lettre de New York.

3. _____ est sur la table?   Un télégramme.

4. _____ est venu?   Madame Dufau.

5. _____ ne fonctionne pas?   Le téléphone.

6. _____ a répondu à la lettre   C'est moi.
   de Monsieur Dupont?

C2. D2. E2.   PRÉCISIONS (*Detailed information*)

Jean-Paul is talking to Sophie about his weekend. Sophie wants more details. Write her questions, using the appropriate interrogative expressions.

Jean-Paul: **Sophie:**

⇨ Je suis sorti avec quelqu'un.   *Avec qui est-ce que tu es sorti?* _____

1. Quelque chose est arrivé.   _____

2. Quelqu'un m'a téléphoné.   _____

3. J'ai rencontré quelqu'un.   _____

4. J'ai fait quelque chose.   _____

5. J'ai joué à quelque chose.   _____

6. Je suis allé au cinéma
    avec quelqu'un.   _____

TRADUCTION

Give the French equivalent of each of the following sentences.

1. *I will send you a card.*

   _____

2. *We will not be able to go to the restaurant.*

   _____

3. *With whom did you go to the movies?*

   _____

4. *What did you talk about?*

   _____

POUR COMMUNIQUER   Une interview

Imagine that a friend of yours went abroad last summer. Ask him six questions about what he did, what and whom he saw, etc. Then report the results of your interview.

_____
_____
_____
_____
_____
_____
_____
_____

UNITÉ 5   MADAME R

Leçon 5   Madame R a dit la vérité!

A1.B1.   VENDREDI 13

Is it dangerous to travel on Friday the thirteenth? The following people are of different opinions. Express everyone's reaction, using the appropriate forms of **croire que** in the present tense.

▷ **Robert / oui**

Robert croit que oui.

1.   Charlotte / non

_____

2.   mes cousins / c'est possible

_____

3.   je / c'est vrai

_____

4.   tu / c'est faux

_____

5.   nous / le vendredi 13 est un jour de chance

_____

6.   vous / les gens sont trop superstitieux

_____

C1.   EN FRANCE

Everyone has his own idea of what he would visit if he were in France. Complete the following sentences with the *conditional* of **visiter**.

▷ **Isabelle** *visiterait* **la Normandie.**

1.   Nous _____ la Provence et la Côte d'Azur.
2.   Charles et Joël _____ Paris.
3.   Henri _____ Marseille.
4.   Tu _____ l'Opéra et la Comédie Française.
5.   Vous _____ la cathédrale de Chartres.
6.   Christine _____ les magasins de mode.
7.   Mes frères _____ Notre-Dame.
8.   Moi, je _____ les plages de Normandie.

C2. LES VACANCES

Read what the following people like or do not like to do during vacation. Say what they *would* do or *would not* do if they were on vacation right now.

▷ **Paul déteste voyager.**

Il ne voyagerait pas.

1. J'aime prendre des photos.

   _____

2. Nous aimons nous promener.

   _____

3. Vous n'aimez pas travailler.

   _____

4. Tu détestes te reposer.

   _____

5. Mes cousins aiment s'amuser.

   _____

6. Philippe déteste se coucher tôt.

   _____

7. Isabelle n'aime pas rester chez elle.

   _____

8. Nous aimons partir en voyage.

   _____

C3. À VINGT ANS

When will you be twenty? In five years? Maybe more or maybe less. Say what you *would* do or *would not* do if you were twenty right now.

▷ habiter chez mes parents?　　*J'habiterais (Je n'habiterais pas) chez mes parents.*

1. aller à l'université? _____

2. aller souvent dans les discothèques? _____

3. avoir une moto? _____

4. avoir une voiture de sport? _____

5. faire des voyages? _____

6. faire du français? _____

7. être indépendant(e)? _____

8. être marié(e)? _____

9. savoir piloter un avion? _____

10. voir mes amis d'aujourd'hui? _____

C4.D1. QUE FAIRE?

Imagine that the people below find themselves in certain situations. Say what they *would* or *would not* do. Use the *conditional* of the expressions in parentheses in *affirmative* or *negative* sentences.

1. Je vois un OVNI (*UFO*). (s'inquiéter? appeler la police? dire bonjour aux extraterrestres?)

_____

_____

_____

2. Nous voyons un accident. (aider les personnes? partir? téléphoner à la police?)

_____

_____

_____

3. Mon meilleur ami est invité à la Maison Blanche. (accepter l'invitation? être un peu nerveux? demander l'autographe du président?)

_____

_____

_____

4. Mes parents gagnent 100.000 dollars à la loterie. (acheter une nouvelle maison? mettre tout l'argent à la banque? donner l'argent à leurs enfants?)

_____

_____

_____

D2. LES BONNES MANIÈRES

Imagine that you are speaking to French friends. Since you are very polite, use the *conditional* of the verbs in parentheses.

1. (vouloir) Je _____ te parler.

   Nous _____ vous inviter.

2. (pouvoir) Est-ce que tu _____ me téléphoner?

   Est-ce que vous _____ passer chez moi?

3. (devoir) Tu _____ être plus patient!

   Vous ne _____ pas être égoïstes!

4. (aimer) J'_____ vous dire quelque chose.

   Mes amis _____ faire votre connaissance.

TRADUCTION

Give the French equivalent of each of the following sentences.

1. *We believe that you are wrong.*

   _____

2. *I am saying that I do not believe you.*

   _____

3. *In my opinion, Jacques will not phone us.*

   _____

4. *With more money, I would go to Tahiti this summer.*

   _____

POUR COMMUNIQUER   L'orage (*The storm*)

Imagine that there is a big storm today. Describe four things you *would do* and four things you *would not do*.

_____

_____

_____

_____

_____

_____

_____

_____

Récréation culturelle

L'été à Menthon-Saint-Bernard

Menthon-Saint-Bernard est un petit village situé (*located*) sur le lac d'Annecy, dans les Alpes françaises.

Imaginez que vous êtes invité(e) à passer quatre semaines à Menthon-Saint-Bernard l'été prochain. Décrivez ce que vous ferez là-bas (excursions, sports, etc. . . .). Utilisez le futur.

GLOSSAIRE: **équitation** *horseback riding* **pêche** *fishing*

_____

_____

_____

_____

_____

Des vacances réussies

Dans cette publicité, un club de voyages, **Résid'Air,** explique le secret des vacances réussies (*successful*). Lisez attentivement cette publicité et répondez aux questions suivantes.

Notre définition des vacances réussies.

Les vacances, c'est le soleil, la mer et les belles plages.

Les vacances, c'est un certain dépaysement (nous vous offrons la Grèce, la Sicile, la Corse, la Tunisie, les Canaries, les Baléares et la Costa del Sol).

Les vacances, c'est avant tout la liberté (nous vous offrons des sports, des distractions, mais rien n'est obligatoire).

Les vacances, c'est avoir le choix (nous vous offrons 4 formules de vacances et plus de 40 destinations pour 7 pays).

Les vacances, c'est découvrir quelque chose de nouveau: du folklore, de la cuisine typique, des objets, des paysages (sur place, nos hôtesses sont là pour vous renseigner et vous conseiller).

Les vacances, c'est partir là où on rêve d'aller (avec le même budget nous vous emmenons plus loin… avec nous, vos vacances vous coûtent vraiment moins cher).

Les vacances, il faut bien les préparer pour les réussir (nous avons préparé pour vous des vacances merveilleuses, elles sont toutes décrites dans notre brochure: demandez-la).

Résid'Air, 83-87, av. d'Italie, Paris 13ᵉ. Tél. (1)45-88-37-85 et 22, rue de l'Arcade, Paris 8ᵉ. Tél. (1)42-65-98-69.

Résid'Air

NOTES DE GÉOGRAPHIE

les Canaries: des îles dans l'Atlantique près de l'Afrique
les Baléares: des îles espagnoles dans la mer Méditerranée
la Costa del Sol: la côte (*coast*) sud-est de l'Espagne

GLOSSAIRE: **dépaysement** *being away from one's usual surroundings*   **découvrir** *to discover*
renseigner *to inform*   **conseiller** *to advise*   **rêver** *to dream*   **emmener** *to take*

Récréation culturelle

1. Qu'est-ce que vous faites quand vous êtes à la plage? _____
_____

2. Aimeriez-vous aller à l'étranger l'été prochain? Quels pays aimeriez-vous visiter? Pourquoi? _____
_____

3. Est-il possible de passer des bonnes vacances si on n'a pas beaucoup d'argent? Comment? _____
_____
_____

4. Quand vous êtes en vacances, est-ce que vous éprouvez le sentiment de liberté (*do you feel free*)?
Comment? _____
_____

5. Quelles sont les choses que vous aimez découvrir pendant les vacances? _____
_____
_____

RÉCRÉEZ-VOUS À MÉGÈVE.

UNITÉ 6: *Les cinq surprises de Paul et de David*

INTRODUCTION: What you will do and learn in *Unité 6*

LESSON OPENERS

Paul and David are two American students who have just arrived in France. Unfortunately, their lack of experience with French customs gets them into a series of misunderstandings.

NOTES CULTURELLES

You will learn about French apartment buildings and about a familiar inhabitant of them (*la concierge*). You will also learn about a world-wide organization devoted to the teaching of French (*l'Alliance Française*), about student housing, and about French wines.

ACTIVITÉS

You will practice how   *pages in your textbook*

STRUCTURE

You will learn the position of double object pronouns, the position of adverbs, and the comparison of adverbs. In this connection you will review several important structures, especially object pronouns, the pronouns *y* and *en*, adverbs in *-ment*, and ordinal numbers.

UNITÉ 6 LES CINQ SURPRISES DE PAUL ET DE DAVID
Leçon 1 Première surprise

A1. À SUIVRE!

Fill in each blank with the appropriate form of **suivre**. This verb must have the same subject and be in the same tense (*present*, **passé composé**, *future*, *imperfect*) as the first verb of that item.

1. Amélie a maigri parce qu'elle _____ un régime très strict.

2. Jacques va à une école de musique où il _____ des cours de piano.

3. Quand nous serons en vacances, nous _____ des cours de ski nautique.

4. J'écoute mes parents mais je ne _____ pas toujours leurs conseils.

5. Quand vous étiez à Paris, est-ce que vous _____ des cours à l'Alliance Française?

6. Venez avec nous! _____-nous!

7. Mes cousins s'intéressent au football. Ils _____ les progrès de leur équipe (*team*) favorite.

8. Mon chien m'obéit. Il me _____ partout (*everywhere*).

9. Nous avons gagné notre match parce que nous _____ les conseils de l'entraîneur (*coach*).

10. Est-ce que tu comprends en classe? Est-ce que tu _____ le professeur?

B1. OUI OU NON?

Read about the following people. Then say what other people do or do not do for them. Use the expressions in parentheses and the appropriate *direct* or *indirect* object pronouns in *affirmative* or *negative* sentences.

▷ **Alain est en voyage. (voir souvent? écrire?)**

Ses amis *ne le voient pas souvent. Ils lui écrivent.*

1. Sylvie organise une boum. (aider? prêter ses disques?)

   Sa cousine _____

2. Jeannette est à l'hôpital. (rendre visite? téléphoner?)

   Son fiancé _____

3. Nos voisins sont des gens très distants. (connaître bien? parler souvent?)

   Nous _____

4. Ce garçon est très snob. (inviter? trouver sympathique?)

   Je _____

5. Le professeur est très intéressant. (répondre? écouter?)

   Les élèves _____

6. Vous avez des idées absurdes. (comprendre? trouver intelligent?)

   Je _____

B2. CONSEILS

Imagine that a French friend talks to you about the following people and things. Give him advice, using the *affirmative* or *negative imperative* forms of the verbs in the box and the appropriate *direct* or *indirect* object pronouns.

votre ami: vous:

▷ **Cette fille est timide.**   *Parle-lui! (Ne lui parle pas!)*

1. Je ne connais pas ce garçon.   _____
2. J'aime bien cette fille.   _____
3. Je trouve ces garçons très snobs.   _____
4. Je voudrais connaître ces filles.   _____
5. Ce garçon dit des choses stupides.   _____
6. Cette revue est bête.   _____
7. Ce programme est intéressant.   _____
8. Ces magazines sont très chers.   _____
9. Mon vélo ne marche (*work*) pas.   _____

acheter
inviter
téléphoner
parler
lire
prendre
vendre
écouter
regarder

B3. S'IL TE PLAÎT!

Imagine that you are talking to your French friend. For each situation, tell him to do or not to do the things in parentheses.

votre situation: vous dites:

▷ **Je ne comprends pas ce problème.**   *Aide-moi!*   (aider)

1. Ce soir je ne serai pas chez moi.   _____ (téléphoner)
2. Je serai chez moi ce week-end.   _____ (rendre visite)
3. Je voudrais aller au cinéma avec toi.   _____ (attendre)
4. Parfois je suis de très mauvaise humeur. _____ (excuser)
5. Demain je ne pourrai pas venir
    au rendez-vous.   _____ (attendre)
6. Je voudrais te parler d'une chose
    importante.   _____ (écouter)

B4. ACCUSATIONS!

Georges accuses his little brother André of many things. André denies them all. Play the role of André using *direct object pronouns*. Make the necessary agreements.

Georges: **André:**

⟹ **Tu as pris ma guitare!**   *Non, je ne l'ai pas prise!* _____

1. Tu as pris mes disques. _____

2. Tu as lu mes lettres! _____

3. Tu as cassé ma calculatrice. _____

4. Tu as regardé mes photos. _____

5. Tu as utilisé ma caméra. _____

6. Tu as mangé mon gâteau. _____

TRADUCTION

Give the French equivalent of each of the following sentences.

1. *See you tomorrow!*

_____

2. *See you next week!*

_____

3. *I will help you if you help me.*

_____

4. *I saw Jeannette but I did not invite her.*

_____

POUR COMMUNIQUER Les voisins

Write six to eight sentences describing your relationships with your neighbors. Use object pronouns.

_____

_____

_____

_____

_____

_____

_____

_____

UNITÉ 6   LES CINQ SURPRISES DE PAUL ET DE DAVID
Leçon 2   Deuxième surprise

VI.   PRÉPOSITIONS

Complete each of the sentences below with a preposition from the box.

contre	
dans	
entre	
jusqu'à	
par	
sans	
sous	
sur	

1.   Nous habitons _____ un immeuble moderne.

2.   Il y a des photos _____ le mur.

3.   Je vais rester chez mon oncle _____ samedi.

4.   Quand nous allons de New York à San Francisco,

     nous passons _____ Denver.

5.   Marc n'est pas riche. Il est souvent _____ argent.

6.   La majorité des femmes sont _____ la discrimination.

7.   La rivière (*river*) passe _____ le pont (*bridge*).

8.   Le Colorado est _____ le Kansas et l'Utah.

A1.   CADEAUX

Read about the following people, and say which gifts people give them. Use an *indirect object* pronoun and the verb **offrir** in the *present* (sentences 1–4) and in the **passé composé** (sentences 5–6).

▷   **Henri aime la musique. Tu** *lui offres un disque* _____ .

1.   Jacqueline aime lire. Je _____ .

2.   Marc n'est pas très ponctuel. Ses parents _____ .

3.   Nos cousins aiment les animaux. Nous _____ .

4.   Votre sœur décore sa chambre. Vous _____ .

5.   Nathalie aime la photo. Son père _____ .

6.   Albert écrit beaucoup. Ses grands-parents _____ .

B1. ÊTES-VOUS GÉNÉREUX (GÉNÉREUSE)?

Imagine that Marc is a French student in your school. You do not know Marc very well, but you know that his friends find him responsible. Marc asks you for the following items. Say whether or not you are going to lend them to him.

▷ votre bicyclette?   *Je la lui prête. (Je ne la lui prête pas.)*

1. votre disque préféré? _____
2. votre nouvelle raquette de tennis? _____
3. les clés de votre maison? _____
4. un dollar? _____
5. cinq dollars? _____
6. vos magazines? _____

B2. D'ACCORD!

Nicole is a very generous person who always says yes to the requests of other people. Express this in *affirmative* sentences, using the verbs in parentheses and *two* object pronouns to replace the nouns in italics.

▷ *Paul* veut *sa bicyclette.*   Nicole *la lui prête* . (prêter)

1. *Monique* veut regarder *les livres.*   Nicole _____ . (prêter)
2. *Henri* veut *son numéro de téléphone.*   Nicole _____ . (donner)
3. *Marc et Éric* veulent écouter *ses disques.*   Nicole _____ . (prêter)
4. *Nathalie* veut regarder *ses photos.*   Nicole _____ . (montrer)
5. *Thomas* veut acheter *sa guitare.*   Nicole _____ . (vendre)
6. *Martine et Claire* veulent savoir *la vérité.*   Nicole _____ . (dire)

B3. OUI!

A French friend asks you if she should do the following things. Tell her to do them. Use *two* object pronouns.

votre amie: **vous:**

▷ Je prête mon vélo à Paul?   *Oui, prête-le-lui!*

1. Je prête mes disques à Catherine? _____
2. Je vends ma guitare à Louis? _____
3. Je montre mes notes (*grades*) à mes parents? _____
4. Je demande ce livre au professeur? _____
5. J'envoie cette lettre à Marc? _____
6. Je donne ce livre à Thérèse? _____

132 Leçon deux

C1. OUI ET NON

Philippe does not always say yes to his friends. Write how he answers their requests, by completing the *affirmative* or *negative* sentences according to the model.

les amis de Philippe:	Philippe:

▷ **Prête-moi ton vélo.**   Non, *je ne te le prête pas* _____ .

1. Prête-moi tes disques.   D'accord, _____ .

2. Prête-nous tes livres.   D'accord, _____ .

3. Vends-moi ta raquette.   Non, _____ .

4. Vends-nous ta moto.   Non, _____ .

5. Montre-moi tes photos.   D'accord, _____ .

6. Donne-nous tes clés.   Non, _____ .

D1. REQUÊTES

Ask a French friend to do the following things for you. Look at the model.

▷ **prêter ta raquette?**   *Prête-la-moi!* _____

1. prêter tes disques?   _____

2. vendre ta calculatrice?   _____

3. montrer tes photos?   _____

4. donner ton numéro de téléphone?   _____

5. raconter cette histoire?   _____

6. rendre mon livre?   _____

TRADUCTION

Give the French equivalent of each of the following sentences.

1. *We live in an apartment building in the suburbs.*

   _____

2. *Who opened this letter?*

   _____

3. *When Paul wants my records, I lend them to him.*

   _____

4. *Do you see that book? Give it to me, please!*

   _____

POUR COMMUNIQUER Emprunts (*Borrowed items*)

Write the names of four friends who have something you are interested in. For each one, say whether he or she lets you use this object. Use the verb **prêter.**

▷ *John a une belle bicyclette, mais il ne me la prête jamais.*

   _____

   _____

   _____

   _____

   _____

   _____

   _____

UNITÉ 6   LES CINQ SURPRISES DE PAUL ET DE DAVID
Leçon 3   Troisième surprise

A1.   QUESTIONS PERSONNELLES

Answer the following questions *affirmatively* or *negatively*. Use the indicated subject pronouns and the pronoun **y**. (Note: The verbs should be in the same tense—*present* or **passé composé**—as in the questions.)

1.   Êtes-vous en classe maintenant?   Je/J' _____ .

     Allez-vous souvent chez vos amis?   Je/J' _____ .

     Êtes-vous allé(e) au Canada?   Je/J' _____ .

2.   Est-ce que votre mère est à la maison? Elle _____ .

     Est-ce qu'elle est allée chez le dentiste
        cette semaine?   Elle _____ .

     Est-ce qu'elle a habité à New York?   Elle _____ .

3.   Vos amis et vous, est-ce que vous allez
        à la plage en été?   Nous _____ .

     Est-ce que vous allez à la piscine
        en hiver?   Nous _____ .

     Est-ce que vous êtes allés au cinéma
        samedi dernier?   Nous _____ .

V1.B1.   OÙ ET QUOI?

Read about the following people. Accordingly, say where they are going and what they are buying there. (In some instances, the people may be going to several places.) You may want to refer to the **Vocabulaire pratique** on pages 304–305 of your textbook.

⇨   **Albert a mal à la tête.**

Il va à la pharmacie. Il achète de l'aspirine.

1.   Nous allons faire un voyage en automobile.

     _____

2.   Je veux laver mon blue-jeans.

     _____

3.   Antoine veut offrir un cadeau à sa fiancée.

     _____

4.   Mes amis veulent faire des sandwichs.

     _____

5.   Hélène veut faire un gâteau.

     _____

C1. UNE VÉGÉTARIENNE

Monique does not eat meat, but she eats everything else. Say whether or not she is having the following foods. Use the verbs in parentheses in *affirmative* or *negative* sentences.

▷ du porc?   *Elle n'en prend pas.* (prendre)

1. de la salade? _____ (prendre)
2. des saucisses? _____ (manger)
3. de la glace? _____ (manger)
4. de l'agneau? _____ (acheter)
5. des croissants? _____ (acheter)
6. du jambon? _____ (commander)

C2. ET VOUS?

Answer the questions below affirmatively or negatively. Use the pronoun **en.**

1. Mangez-vous souvent de la glace?

_____

2. Buvez-vous de l'eau minérale?

_____

3. Achetez-vous du chocolat?

_____

4. Faites-vous de la gymnastique?

_____

5. Faites-vous du ski nautique?

_____

6. Avez-vous de l'énergie maintenant?

_____

7. Avez-vous des projets pour demain?

_____

8. Gagnez-vous de l'argent en été?

_____

C3.   **EN FRANCE**

The following people went to France this summer and did certain things. Say that they have *never* done these things before. Follow the model.

▷   **Charles a fait du ski nautique.**

Il n'en a jamais fait avant.

1.   Christine a mangé des croissants.

2.   Nous avons commandé des escargots (*snails*).

3.   Mon cousin a bu du champagne.

4.   Hélène a acheté du parfum français.

5.   Vous avez fait de la planche à voile.

C4.   **CONSEILS**

Brigitte wants to lose weight. She asks you if she should do the following. Answer her *affirmatively* or *negatively*.

▷   **Je mange des spaghetti?**   *Non, n'en mange pas!*

1.   Je mange des fruits?

2.   Je mange de la glace?

3.   Je bois de l'eau minérale?

4.   Je bois de la bière?

5.   Je fais du sport?

TRADUCTION

Give the French equivalent of each of the following sentences.

1. *Pierre is at the movies, but Henri is not (there).*

   _____

2. *I like that restaurant. We have dinner there often.*

   _____

3. *We like cheese. We eat some every day.*

   _____

4. *Here is some aspirin. Take some!*

   _____

POUR COMMUNIQUER   Préférences

Make a list of six foods you like very much. Say whether you have them at home or at school.

_____

_____

_____

_____

_____

_____

_____

_____

UNITÉ 6   LES CINQ SURPRISES DE PAUL ET DE DAVID
Leçon 4   Quatrième surprise

A1.   EXPRESSION PERSONNELLE

Read the sentences below, and rewrite them with one of the following *expressions of quantity*. Your sentences may be *affirmative* or *negative*.

peu / assez / beaucoup / trop

▷ **Nous avons des examens.**

Nous avons trop d'examens.
(Nous n'avons pas assez d'examens.)

1.   Le professeur donne des exercises.

_____

2.   Mes parents ont de la patience.

_____

3.   Les jeunes Américains ont des responsabilités.

_____

4.   Nous mangeons des produits artificiels.

_____

5.   Il y a des programmes intéressants à la télé.

_____

6.   Les Américains consomment de l'énergie.

_____

7.   Les voitures japonaises consomment de l'essence.

_____

B1. ET VOUS?

Caroline is speaking about herself. Say whether or not you do the same things, using an *expression of quantity* in your response.

Caroline: **vous:**

▷ **Je fais du sport**   *Moi, j'en fais beaucoup.*
                                (Je n'en fais pas assez.)

1. Je fais des progrès en français. _____
2. J'ai des disques de musique reggae. _____
3. Je gagne de l'argent. _____
4. J'achète des magazines. _____
5. Je fais du jogging. _____
6. J'ai des examens. _____

V1. AU MARCHÉ (At the market)

Imagine that you are spending a month in France with your family. Since you speak French, you are doing the shopping at the local market. Ask for the following items, specifying the quantity you want. Use nouns from the **Vocabulaire pratique** on page 311 of your textbook.

▷ (des oranges)   *S'il vous plaît, donnez-moi un sac (deux kilos) d'oranges.*

1. (des bananes) _____
2. (de l'eau minérale) _____
3. (de la lessive) _____
4. (de la moutarde) _____
5. (du vin) _____
6. (du fromage) _____
7. (du vinaigre) _____
8. (du thé) _____

C1. SOLDES! (Sale!)

There is a record sale going on, and each record is selling for 16 francs. Say how many records the following students are buying with their money.

▷ **Daniel a 32 francs.**   *Il en achète deux.*

1. Marie a 80 francs. _____
2. Nous avons 320 francs. _____
3. Tu as 16 francs. _____
4. J'ai 96 francs. _____
5. Mes cousins ont 160 francs. _____

C2. COMBIEN?

Say whether or not you have the items in sentences 1–3. Say *how many* of the items in sentences 4–6 you have.

▷ un chien? *Oui, j'en ai un. (Non, je n'en ai pas.)*

1. un chat? _____

2. un téléviseur? _____

3. une bicyclette? _____

4. des disques? _____

5. des cousins? _____

6. des cousines? _____

D1. OUI OU NON?

Jacques is telling you what he does. Say whether or not you do the same things. Use *two* object pronouns in your responses.

Jacques: **vous:**

▷ **J'écris des lettres à ma cousine.**   *Je (ne) lui en écris (pas).*

1. Je demande de l'argent à mes parents. _____

2. Je donne des conseils à mes amis. _____

3. Je donne du sucre à mon chien. _____

4. J'envoie des cartes d'anniversaire à mes amies. _____

TRADUCTION

Give the French equivalent of each of the following sentences.

1. *You eat too much bread.*

   _____

2. *How much does this book cost?*

   _____

3. *Hélène has two brothers. I have one.*

   _____

4. *Do you have any apples? Give me two!*

   _____

POUR COMMUNIQUER   Vos possessions

List some of your belongings, and say whether your brother or sister has the same items.

▷ *J'ai une calculatrice. Ma sœur en a une aussi.*

_____

_____
_____
_____
_____
_____
_____
_____

UNITÉ 6   LES CINQ SURPRISES DE PAUL ET DE DAVID
Leçon 5   Cinquième (et dernière) surprise

A1.   SUPER-MARATHON

Some of your friends participated in the Super-Marathon. Now the race is over, and you are writing down the results. Use the appropriate *ordinal* numbers.

▷ **André (3)**   *André est troisième.* _____

1. Sylvie (7)   _____

2. Arthur (10)   _____

3. Simon (11)   _____

4. Roger (20)   _____

5. Michèle (33)   _____

6. Marc (100)   _____

B1.   UNE QUESTION DE TEMPÉRAMENT

Read about the following people, and say that they act according to their personalities. Use the verbs in parentheses and the appropriate adverbs in **-ment.**

▷ **Pierre est nerveux. (conduire)**   *Il conduit nerveusement.* _____

1. Michèle est sérieuse. (travailler)   _____

2. Paul est calme. (répondre)   _____

3. Charles est impulsif. (faire tout)   _____

4. Albert est rationnel.
   (analyser ce problème)   _____

5. Thomas est patient. (attendre)   _____

6. Philippe est intelligent. (parler)   _____

7. Nathalie est brillante. (écrire)   _____

C1.   NICOLE ET ALAIN

Nicole wants to know more about Alain. Read Nicole's questions and write Alain's answers, using the adverbs in parentheses. (Do not use object pronouns in your answers.)

Nicole: **Alain:**

▷ **Tu aimes le jazz?**   Oui, *j'aime beaucoup le jazz* _____ . (beaucoup)

1. Tu aimes la musique
   classique?   Non, _____ . (beaucoup)

2. Tu joues au tennis?   Oui, _____ . (bien)

3. Tu écris à tes parents?   Non, _____ . (souvent)

4. Tu es heureux ici?   Oui, _____ . (généralement)

5. Tu vas à tes classes?   Non, _____ . (toujours)

C2. POURQUOI?

Read what happened to the following people. Then explain why these things happened, by using the **passé composé** of the verbs in parentheses and one of the following adverbs: **bien / mal / trop / beaucoup.**

▷ Je suis fatigué. (travailler) *J'ai beaucoup (trop) travaillé.*

1. Vous avez perdu le match. (jouer) _____

2. Nous avons gagné. (jouer) _____

3. Jacques est malade. (manger) _____

4. Tu es reposé. (dormir) _____

5. Charlotte a gagné le débat. (parler) _____

6. Vous connaissez des choses très intéressantes. (lire) _____

D1. PLUS OU MOINS?

Make comparisons using the given elements and the adverb in **-ment** derived from the adjective in italics.

▷ ma mère / conduire / *rapide* / mon père
Ma mère conduit plus (moins, aussi) rapidement que mon père.

1. je / étudier / *sérieux* / mes amis

_____

2. les jeunes / travailler / *énergique* / les vieux

_____

3. les gens du Nord / parler / *lent* / les gens du Sud

_____

4. les femmes / conduire / *prudent* / les hommes

_____

TRADUCTION

Give the French equivalent of each of the following sentences.

1. *At present, I am at home.* _____

2. *Fortunately, we have enough money.* _____

3. *Pierre often plays tennis with us.* _____

4. *I did not like this book very much.* _____

POUR COMMUNIQUER   Préférences

Describe five things you like to do. Say how well and how often you do them.

_____

_____

_____

_____

_____

Récréation culturelle

La carte d'identité scolaire

La majorité des élèves français ont une «carte d'identité scolaire». Cette carte leur donne de nombreux (*numerous*) avantages. Avec une carte d'identité scolaire, on obtient (*get*) des réductions sur le prix des billets de cinéma, de théâtre, de concerts et de musées. On paie moins cher quand on voyage en train ou en autobus.

Regardez cette carte d'identité scolaire.

1. Comment s'appelle cette élève? _____

2. Où habite-t-elle? _____

3. Quel est le nom de l'établissement scolaire où elle étudie?

_____

Unité 6

Récréation culturelle

À *l'Institut de Touraine*

L'Institut de Touraine est une école pour les étudiants qui désirent se perfectionner (*to improve*) en français. Cette école est située (*located*) à Tours, une ville du centre de la France.

Imaginez que vous allez passer un mois à Tours l'été prochain. Vous décidez de suivre des cours à l'Institut de Touraine. Remplissez le bulletin d'inscription (*registration form*).

UNIVERSITÉ DE TOURS

INSTITUT D'ETUDES FRANÇAISES
DE TOURAINE
POUR LES ETRANGERS
1, Rue de la Grandière, 37000 TOURS

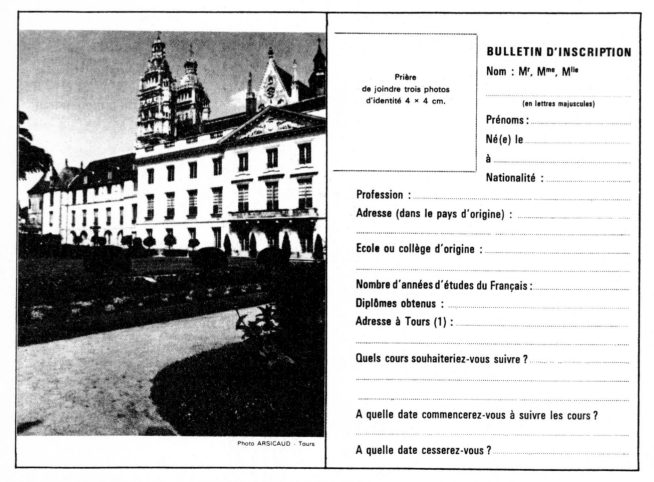

Photo ARSICAUD - Tours

Prière
de joindre trois photos
d'identité 4 × 4 cm.

BULLETIN D'INSCRIPTION

Nom : M^r, Mme, Mlle

....
(en lettres majuscules)

Prénoms : ....

Né(e) le ....

à ....

Nationalité : ....

Profession : ....

Adresse (dans le pays d'origine) : ....

....

Ecole ou collège d'origine : ....

....

Nombre d'années d'études du Français : ....

Diplômes obtenus : ....

Adresse à Tours (1) : ....

Quels cours souhaiteriez-vous suivre ? ....

....

A quelle date commencerez-vous à suivre les cours ?

A quelle date cesserez-vous ? ....

GLOSSAIRE: **obtenus** *obtained* **souhaiteriez** *would you like* **cesserez** *will you stop*

Récréation culturelle

Une soirée à la Cité Universitaire (A party at the students' residence)

Un grand nombre d'étudiants étrangers qui habitent à Paris vivent à la Cité Universitaire.
La soirée mentionnée dans le prospectus suivant a été organisée par les étudiants américains
de la Cité Universitaire.

Lisez ce prospectus:

FONDATION DES ÉTATS-UNIS

SOIRÉE DANSANTE AVEC BUFFET

PÂTÉS, FROMAGES, VINS EN TONNEAUX

SAMEDI, 8 MARS DE 21H À 1H DANS LA CAFÉTÉRIA

Contrôle à l'entrée: n'oubliez pas votre carte
de résidence

GLOSSAIRE: **tonneaux** *casks*

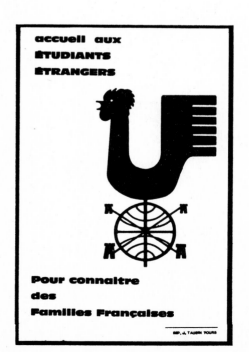

accueil aux
ÉTUDIANTS
ÉTRANGERS

Pour connaître
des
Familles Françaises

1. Qu'est-ce que c'est qu'une «soirée dansante»?

    _____

2. Quelle est la date de cette soirée?

    _____

3. Qu'est-ce qu'il y a à manger?

    _____

4. Qu'est-ce qu'il y a à boire?

UNITÉ 7: *Quelle soirée!*

INTRODUCTION: What you will do and learn in *Unité 7*

LESSON OPENERS

Olivier has invited Mireille to the big concert. To create a good impression, he would like to pick her up in his father's new car . . . but that decision is going to create certain problems for him.

NOTES CULTURELLES

You will learn about the musical tastes of young French people, about the role of the father in the French family, and about French cars.

ACTIVITÉS

You will practice how   *pages in your textbook*

STRUCTURE

You will learn a new verb form: the subjunctive. Although the subjunctive has all but disappeared from English, it is used frequently in French.

UNITÉ 7   QUELLE SOIRÉE!
Leçon 1   Une invitation

A1.   VERBES

Read the following sentences. Then fill in each blank with the verb that fits logically. The verb in the second sentence of each item must be in the same tense (*present* or **passé composé**) as the verb in the first sentence.

▷ **Ce livre n'est pas à moi. Il** _appartient_ **à Robert.**

tenir	
appartenir	
obtenir	
retenir	
se tenir	

1.   Nous faisons des progrès en tennis. Nous _____ à un excellent club.

2.   Tu étudies beaucoup. Tu _____ des bonnes notes.

3.   Bernard est un enfant très poli. Il _____ bien à table.

4.   Vous êtes honnête. Vous _____ toujours vos promesses.

5.   Nous sommes allés au théâtre. Nous _____ deux billets pour samedi.

6.   Alain a téléphoné au docteur Belcour. Il _____ un rendez-vous.

7.   Mon petit frère n'a pas parlé. Il _____ tranquille pendant le concert.

B1.   CONTENT?

Read what the following people are doing, and say whether or not they are happy doing these things.

▷ **Antoine sort avec sa cousine. Il** _(n') est (pas) content de sortir avec sa cousine_ .

1.   Je pars en vacances. Je _____ .

2.   Vous avez un examen lundi. Vous _____ .

3.   Ma meilleure amie va à Paris. Elle _____ .

4.   Nous voyons nos amis. Nous _____ .

5.   Tu as un «A» à l'examen. Tu _____ .

6.   Olivier a un «F». Il _____ .

B2.   EXPRESSION PERSONNELLE

Say how you feel about the things you do. Complete each sentence with an expression of your choice.

▷ **Je suis heureux (heureuse)** _d'avoir des amis sympathiques (d'aller en vacances, de sortir le week-end ...)_

1.   Je ne suis pas heureux (heureuse) _____ .

2.   Je suis fatigué(e) _____ .

3.   Chez moi, je suis obligé(e) _____ .

4.   En classe, je suis obligé(e) _____ .

5.   Chez moi, je suis libre (*free*) _____ .

6.   Je ne suis pas libre _____ .

C1. OPINIONS

Read about the activities of the following people, and give your opinions about them. Use the adjectives below in *impersonal expressions*.

bon / mauvais / amusant / agréable / ennuyeux / pénible / facile / difficile / dangereux / utile / inutile / important / ridicule

▷ Jacqueline conduit vite. *Il est dangereux (Il n'est pas amusant) de conduire vite.*

1. Charles voyage souvent. _____

2. Albert perd son temps. _____

3. Thomas gaspille son argent. _____

4. Nicole suit des classes de karaté. _____

5. Hélène fait du jogging. _____

6. Suzanne critique ses amis. _____

7. Jean-Louis s'inquiète souvent. _____

8. Marie-Laure est souvent malade. _____

9. Alice apprend l'espagnol. _____

10. Guillaume aide ses parents. _____

TRADUCTION

Give the French equivalent of each of the following sentences.

1. *This bicycle belongs to my brother.*

   _____

2. *I am tired of studying.*

   _____

3. *We are happy to invite your friends.*

   _____

4. *It is not necessary to wait for Pierre.*

   _____

POUR COMMUNIQUER   Dans la vie (*In life*)

What are the important things in life and the less important ones? Express your opinions by completing the sentences below.

Il est important _____ .

Il est utile _____ .

Il est dangereux _____ .

Il n'est pas nécessaire _____ .

Il est bon _____ .

UNITÉ 7 QUELLE SOIRÉE!
Leçon 2 Déception et décision

A1. AVANT L'EXAMEN

The French teacher wants the students to finish certain assignments before their test. Express this by filling in each of the blanks below with the appropriate form of the *subjunctive* of **finir**.

1. Le professeur veut que nous _____ ce livre.

2. Il veut que tu _____ ces exercices.

3. Il veut que Charles _____ ce projet.

4. Il veut que Marc et Hélène _____ ces préparations.

5. Il veut que vous _____ cette leçon.

6. Il veut que je _____ ce chapitre.

A2. CHEZ LE MÉDECIN

The following people are having their annual checkup. Say that the doctor does not want them to continue what they are doing. Complete each of the sentences with the *subjunctive* form of the expression in italics.

1. Robert *travaille trop*.   Le médecin ne veut pas qu'il _____ .

2. Thomas *s'énerve*.   Le médecin ne veut pas qu'il _____ .

3. Valérie *maigrit*.   Le médecin ne veut pas qu'elle _____ .

4. Jacques *grossit*.   Le médecin ne veut pas qu'il _____ .

5. Anne *prend trop d'aspirine*.   Le médecin ne veut pas qu'elle _____

_____ .

6. Isabelle *dort trop*.   Le médecin ne veut pas qu'elle _____ .

7. Mon père *lit sans lunettes*.   Le médecin ne veut pas qu'il _____

_____ .

8. M. Goulot *boit beaucoup de bière*. Le médecin ne veut pas qu'il _____

_____ .

L'ENTRAÎNEUR (*The coach*)

Imagine that you are the coach for a French tennis team. Tell the players what you expect from them. Begin your sentences with **Je veux** or **Je ne veux pas** and use the **vous** form of the subjunctive.

▷ jouer mal?   *Je ne veux pas que vous jouiez mal!*

1. jouer bien?   _____

2. gagner?   _____

3. perdre?   _____

4. perdre votre temps?   _____

5. maigrir?   _____

6. grossir?   _____

7. vous reposer avant
   le match?   _____
        _____

8. vous impatienter pendant
   le match?   _____

A4.   OUI OU NON?

Often people have certain expectations for us. Say what expectations the following people have placed on you. Complete each of the sentences below with **veut** or **ne veut pas** and the **je** form of the subjunctive of a verb from the box.

1. Mon père _____
   _____ .

2. Ma mère _____
   _____ .

3. Le professeur _____
   _____ .

4. Mon meilleur ami _____
   _____

5. Ma meilleure amie _____
   _____ .

6. Le voisin _____
   _____ .

| réussir à l'examen |
| obéir |
| quitter l'école |
| l'aider |
| le/la critiquer |
| lui téléphoner |

B1. NON!

The following people do not want other people to take certain objects. Express this by using the present of **vouloir** and the *subjunctive* of **prendre.**

▷ **je (tu / ma caméra)**

Je ne veux pas que tu prennes ma caméra.

1. Henri (son frère / son vélo)

_____

2. mes parents (je / la voiture)

_____

3. vous (nous / vos disques)

_____

4. tu (tes cousins / ta moto)

_____

5. Claire (vous / ses photos)

_____

6. Georges (tu / sa guitare)

_____

B2. ZUT ALORS!

There are many things that we cannot do because other people do not let us do them. Express this by completing each of the sentences below with the present of **vouloir** and the *subjunctive* of the verb in italics, according to the model.

▷ Je veux *sortir* mais mes parents *ne veulent pas que je sorte* _____ .

1. Hélène veut *conduire* mais son frère _____ sa voiture.

2. Vous voulez *partir* mais vos amis _____ .

3. Les élèves veulent *dormir,* mais le professeur _____ en classe.

4. Éric veut *boire* du champagne, mais sa mère _____ du vin!

B3. SOUHAITS (*Wishes*)

Express the wishes of the people below by using elements from columns A, B, and C.

A	B	C	
désirer	je	dire la vérité	organiser une boum
vouloir	tu	obéir	trouver un job intéressant
préférer	nous	maigrir	gagner de l'argent
	vous	apprendre le français	écrire pendant les vacances
	mes/ses/leurs amis		
	les jeunes		

▷ Vous *désirez que j'écrive pendant les vacances* .

1. Je _____ .

2. Nous _____ .

3. Le professeur _____ .

4. Le médecin _____ .

5. Mes parents _____ .

6. Mes amis _____ .

7. Les adultes _____ .

8. Tu _____ .

TRADUCTION

Give the French equivalent of each of the following sentences.

1. *I want you to come at ten.*

   _____

2. *Do you want me to call?*

   _____

3. *My father does not want me to drive his car.*

   _____

4. *I do not want you to read this letter.*

   _____

ENTRE NOUS Souhaits (*Wishes*)

Express your wishes for the following people.

Je voudrais que mon meilleur ami _____ .

Je voudrais que ma meilleure amie _____ .

Je ne veux pas que mes amis _____ .

Je désire que mes voisins _____ .

J'aimerais que mes parents _____ .

UNITÉ 7   QUELLE SOIRÉE!
Leçon 3   Catastrophe!

A1.B1.   **RIEN N'EST PARFAIT!** (*Nothing's perfect!*)

It's difficult to satisfy everyone. Express this by completing each of the sentences below with the appropriate *subjunctive* form of the verb in italics.

▷ Je *suis* un excellent athlète. Mes professeurs aimeraient _*que je sois*_ un excellent étudiant.

1. Paul *a* une moto. Sa fiancée aimerait _____ une voiture.

2. Vous *êtes* indépendant. Vos parents aimeraient _____ moins individualiste.

3. Mes parents *sont* sympathiques. J'aimerais _____ plus généreux avec moi.

4. Nous *avons* un «B» à l'examen. Le professeur aimerait _____ un «A».

5. Tu *es* au café. Ton père aimerait _____ à la maison.

6. Mes amis *ont* une vieille voiture. J'aimerais _____ une voiture de sport.

7. Vous *avez* de l'imagination. Vos parents aimeraient _____ de l'ambition.

8. J'*ai* des disques de musique classique. Mon cousin aimerait _____ des disques de jazz.

C1.   **APRÈS LE CONCERT**

After the concert, everyone says why they must leave. Express this idea, beginning your sentences with **Il faut que.**

▷ Je dois partir.   _*Il faut que je parte.*_

1. Nous devons rentrer.   _____

2. Tu dois prendre un taxi.   _____

3. Marc doit passer chez son frère.   _____

4. Vous devez téléphoner chez vous.   _____

5. Sophie et Claire doivent partir.   _____

6. Je dois accompagner Suzanne.   _____

C2. QUE FAIRE?

Analyze the following situations, and write what the people should or should not do. Begin each of your sentences with **Il faut que** or **Il ne faut pas que** and use the *subjunctive* of the expression in parentheses.

▷ Jacques a beaucoup grossi. (manger des spaghetti? maigrir?)

Il ne faut pas qu'il mange des spaghetti. Il faut qu'il maigrisse.

1. Henri a un rendez-vous avec une amie qui n'est pas à l'heure. (partir? être patient? sortir avec une autre fille?)

   _____
   _____

2. Philippe a cassé le nouveau walkman de son frère. (inventer une histoire? dire la vérité? s'excuser?)

   _____
   _____

3. Mes parents veulent aller au cinéma mais il y a une tempête de neige (*snowstorm*). (sortir? prendre un taxi? rester à la maison?)

   _____
   _____

4. Je veux aller au restaurant avec mes amis ce week-end, mais je n'ai pas d'argent. (vendre mon livre de français? demander de l'argent à mes parents? rester chez moi?)

   _____
   _____

5. Nous sommes dans un hôtel qui brûle (*is burning*). (être calmes? être nerveux? appeler la police?)

   _____
   _____

D1. L'AMI IDÉAL

What are the characteristics of the ideal friend? Indicate whether the following are important or not. Begin each of your sentences with **Il est (très, assez) important que** or **Il n'est pas (très) important que** + *subjunctive*.

▷ être intelligent?

Il (n') est (pas) très important qu'il soit intelligent.

1. être sincère? _____

2. avoir de l'argent? _____

3. avoir le sens de l'humour? _____

4. dire la vérité? _____

5. comprendre mes problèmes? _____

6. être toujours d'accord avec moi? _____

D2. CONSEILS MÉDICAUX (*Medical advice*)

Imagine that you are a doctor practicing medicine in France. Give your opinions about the following people's habits. Begin each of your sentences with **Il est bon que** or **Il n'est pas bon que.**

▷   **Vous mangez trop.**   *Il n'est pas bon que vous mangiez trop.*

1.   Vous mangez beaucoup de fruits.   _____

2.   M. Thomas boit trop de bière.   _____

3.   Ce garçon grossit.   _____

4.   Robert dort mal.   _____

5.   Vous vous énervez.   _____

6.   Vous nagez tous les jours.   _____

D3. OUI OU NON?

Express your feelings about the following by using the adjectives in parentheses in *affirmative* or *negative* sentences.

▷   **les jeunes / avoir des responsabilités? (normal)**

Il est normal (Il n'est pas normal) que les jeunes aient des responsabilités.

1.   les femmes d'aujourd'hui / être indépendantes? (bon)

_____

_____

2.   nous / aider nos parents? (naturel)

_____

3.   nos parents / être généreux avec nous? (nécessaire)

_____

_____

4.   les jeunes Américains / apprendre des langues (*languages*) étrangères? (utile)

_____

_____

5.   les Américains / développer l'énergie nucléaire? (absurde)

_____

_____

TRADUCTION

Give the French equivalent of each of the following sentences.

1. *I know that you are learning Spanish.*

   _____

2. *I want you to learn French.*

   _____

3. *It is too bad that Pierre is not with us.*

   _____

4. *It would be better that you call Antoine.*

   _____

POUR COMMUNIQUER   Réflexions personnelles

Express your opinion about yourself or people you know. Complete the following sentences.

Il est important que _____ .

Il n'est pas nécessaire que _____ .

Il est utile que _____ .

Il est dommage que _____ .

Il vaudrait mieux que _____ .

UNITÉ 7 QUELLE SOIRÉE!
Leçon 4 Tout s'arrange!

A1. **L'OURAGAN** (*The hurricane*)

A dangerous hurricane has been predicted for this weekend. Say whether or not the people below should do the following things. Begin each of your sentences with **Il faut que** or **Il ne faut pas que.**

1. ma mère / faire les courses aujourd'hui?

    _____

2. toi / faire du camping samedi?

    _____

3. nous / aller à la plage ce week-end?

    _____

4. moi / aller au supermarché ce matin?

    _____

5. les automobilistes (*drivers*) / faire très attention?

    _____

6. vous / faire de la voile dimanche?

    _____

7. ma cousine / aller chez ses amis ce week-end?

    _____

B1. **ANNETTE**

Read about the people in Annette's life, and say whether or not she is happy about them. Begin each of your sentences with **Elle est contente que** or **Elle n'est pas contente que.**

1. Ses parents sont généreux.

    _____

2. Sa meilleure amie va au Canada cet été.

    _____

3. Son frère ne dit pas la vérité.

    _____

4. Son petit ami a une voiture de sport.

    _____

5. Son petit ami sort avec d'autres (*other*) filles.

    _____

B2. EFFET DOUBLE

The following events cause two people (or groups of people) to be happy or unhappy. In completing the sentences select the *infinitive* or the *subjunctive* construction as appropriate.

▷ **Nancy a une voiture.**

Nancy est heureuse *d'avoir une voiture* .

Jean-Pierre est heureux *qu'elle ait une voiture* .

1. Je suis malade.

   J'ai peur _____ .

   Ma mère a peur _____ .

2. Vous visitez Paris.

   Je suis content _____ .

   Vous êtes contents _____ .

3. Caroline a des amies françaises.

   Caroline est heureuse _____ .

   Ses parents sont heureux _____ .

4. Nous partons.

   Nos amis sont tristes _____ .

   Nous sommes tristes _____ .

TRADUCTION

Give the French equivalent of each of the following sentences.

1. *My parents want me to go to France.*

   _____

2. *I am happy that you are coming to my house.*

   _____

3. *Pierre is afraid that his friends are not coming.*

   _____

4. *Are you happy that I am writing to you?*

   _____

POUR COMMUNIQUER Vos sentiments

Express your feelings towards the actions of other people. Complete the sentences below.

▷ **Je suis heureux (heureuse) que** *mes amis me comprennent* .

Je suis triste que _____ .

Je suis surpris(e) que _____ .

Je suis fier (fière) que _____ .

J'ai peur que _____ .

UNITÉ 7   QUELLE SOIRÉE!
Leçon 5   Sauvé? Pas tout à fait!

V1.   POURQUOI PAS?

Say that the following people did not go to the places they were supposed to go, and explain why. Use **parce que** or **à cause de** as appropriate.

▷   **Henri / au cinéma / la neige**

Henri n'est pas allé au cinéma à cause de la neige.

▷   **Sylvie / au concert / il neigeait**

Sylvie n'est pas allée au concert parce qu'il neigeait.

1.   je / chez mes amis / l'examen

   _____

2.   nous / à la plage / le mauvais temps

   _____

3.   Philippe / au restaurant avec nous / son rendez-vous avec Annie

   _____

   _____

4.   Thomas / à la piscine / il était malade

   _____

5.   vous / au théâtre / vous avez dû étudier

   _____

A1.   OÙ EST HENRI?

Henri is traveling through Europe. The last letter he sent came from Paris. Some of his friends think he is still in Paris, others don't. Complete the sentences accordingly.

▷   **Claude pense** *qu'il est à Paris* _____ .

▷   **Françoise n'est pas sûre** *qu'il soit à Paris* _____ .

1.   Je crois _____ .

2.   Thérèse ne pense pas _____ .

3.   Josiane ne croit pas _____ .

4.   Croyez-vous _____ ?

5.   Michel n'est pas sûr _____ .

6.   Nous pensons _____ .

A2. L'ÉCOLE BUISSONNIÈRE (*Playing hooky*)

Pierre and his friends have decided to cut classes, but the principal has doubts about the validity of their excuses. Write the principal's reactions, beginning each statement with **Je doute que.**

les amis de Pierre: le directeur:

⇨ **Pierre est malade.**   *Je doute que Pierre soit malade.*

1. Jacques va chez le médecin.   _____

2. Hélène et Suzanne vont chez le dentiste.   _____

3. Paul a un examen médical.   _____

4. Henri et Albert ont un problème sérieux.   _____

5. Marc est à l'hôpital.   _____

6. Irène et Sylvie ont la grippe (*flu*).   _____

A3. LES CINQ ERREURS D'HENRI

Henri wrote the following essay on the United States in which he made five mistakes. Use the model to point out his errors.

Henri a écrit: Les États-Unis sont un grand pays. Au nord, il y a le Canada. Au sud, il y a le Venezuela. La capitale des États-Unis est New York. New York est une ville immense avec des grandes avenues et un grand parc. La Statue de la Liberté est située (*located*) dans ce grand parc. New York est à l'est. San Francisco est à l'ouest. On met trois heures en avion pour aller de New York à San Francisco. Disneyland est la grande attraction de cette ville.

Erreur numéro 1: Es-tu sûr *qu'au sud il y ait le Venezuela* _____ ?

Erreur numéro 2: Crois-tu _____ ?

Erreur numéro 3: Es-tu certain _____ ?

Erreur numéro 4: Penses-tu _____ ?

Erreur numéro 5: Je doute _____ .

B1.   MADAME MARTIN

Madame Martin is speaking to her son André. Complete each of her sentences with the *indicative* or *subjunctive* form of the verbs in parentheses.

1. (être / aller)   Je pense que tu _____ malade.

    J'aimerais que tu _____ chez le médecin.

2. (faire / être)   Je doute que tu _____ des progrès en anglais.

    Je crois que tu _____ un peu paresseux.

3. (être / aller)   Je voudrais que tu _____ médecin.

    Il faut que tu _____ à l'université.

4. (penser / écrire)   Je suis sûr que tu _____ souvent à ton grand-père.

    Il est important que tu lui _____ une carte pour son anniversaire.

B2.   EXPRESSION PERSONNELLE

Say how you feel about the following situations. Begin your sentences with expressions such as
**je suis sûr(e) que / je sais que / je doute que / il faut que / il est important que / je voudrais que /
je suis heureux (heureuse) que . . .**

1. Mon meilleur ami est très riche.

    _____

2. Mes parents sont tolérants.

    _____

3. Les jeunes sont indépendants.

    _____

4. Le président est intelligent.

    _____

5. Ma famille me comprend.

    _____

6. Nous allons au Canada cet été.

TRADUCTION

Give the French equivalent of each of the following sentences.

1. *Marie is studying tonight because of the exam.*

   _____

2. *I know that Pierre is nice, but I doubt that he is very intelligent.*

   _____

   _____

3. *Are you sure that Charlotte is sick?*

   _____

4. *I am happy to go to the movies, but I am sad that you are not coming with us.*

   _____

   _____

POUR COMMUNIQUER   Croyances (*Beliefs*)

Describe three things that you believe and three things that you do not believe.

_____

_____

_____

_____

_____

_____

_____

_____

Récréation culturelle

Une petite économique

Lisez la publicité et répondez aux questions suivantes.

Champion de France dès la 1ère année

RENAULT 21.

Accélerations 0 à 100 km/h: 9,7 s

Vitesse maximum: 217 km/h

Consommation aux 100 km:
6,7 litres à 90 km/h
8,1 litres à 120 km/h
10,8 litres en ville

Prix: À partir de 90.000 F

Vive le sport

RENAULT
DES VOITURES
À VIVRE

GLOSSAIRE: **À partir de** *Starting at*

1. Quelle est la marque de cette voiture? _____

2. Quel est son prix en francs français? _____

3. Quelle est sa consommation d'essence (en litres par 100 kilomètres) à la vitesse (*speed*) de

   120 kilomètres/heure? _____

4. Aimeriez-vous conduire cette voiture? Pourquoi? (Pourquoi pas?) _____

   _____

Unité 7

Récréation culturelle

Sur la route

Si vous voyagez en France en auto, vous verrez les panneaux de signalisation (*traffic signs*) suivants. Lisez leur signification (*meaning*) en français et donnez l'équivalent anglais.

1.  Sens interdit.

_____

5. Interdiction de doubler.

_____

_____

2.  Interdiction de tourner à gauche.

_____

6. Vitesse limitée à 50 kilomètres à l'heure.

_____

_____

3.  Interdiction de tourner à droite.

_____

7. Fin de vitesse limitée à 60 kilomètres à l'heure.

_____

_____

4.  Interdiction de faire demi-tour.

_____

8.  Fin d'interdiction de doubler.

_____

_____

Vous avez la parole

Regardez le dessin suivant et décrivez la situation.

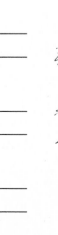

1. Où se passe la scène?

_____

_____

2. Quel est le problème?

_____

_____

3. Qu'est-ce qui est arrivé?

_____

_____

Récréation culturelle

Vive la musique!

Depuis quelques années, Paris a un Palais Omnisports à Bercy (un quartier de Paris) où 17.000 spectateurs peuvent assister à des réunions (*meetings*) sportives ou à des concerts. Les jeunes, en particulier, vont à Bercy pour écouter leurs idoles de rock.

1. Quel groupe va donner un concert à Bercy? _____

2. Quelle est la date de leur concert? _____

3. À quelle heure commence le concert? _____

4. Quel est votre groupe de rock favori? _____

   Êtes-vous allé(e) à leurs concerts? _____

   Où et quand? _____

UNITÉ 8: *Camping*

INTRODUCTION: What you will do and learn in *Unité 8*

LESSON OPENERS

Jacques, Bernard, and Roger, three French teenagers, are going camping in southern France. Their trip starts out well, but soon the boys run into difficulties . . .

NOTES CULTURELLES

You will read about how the French spend their summer vacations, about camping and the French countryside, and about the attitudes of young French people toward military service.

ACTIVITÉS

You will practice how   *pages in your textbook*

to talk about the outdoors 389–390
to say that you are learning (beginning, trying, etc.) to do
 certain things 392–393
to describe what you can see in the sky 397
to describe two actions taking place at the same time 403
to describe a relationship of cause and effect 403–404

STRUCTURE

You will learn about the infinitive, which is used frequently in French. You will learn a new verb form: the present participle. And you will learn two new pronouns: the interrogative pronoun (*lequel*) and the demonstrative pronoun (*celui*).

UNITÉ 8 CAMPING
Leçon 1 Préparatifs

V1. CAMPING

The following people are camping. Read what they are doing, and complete each sentence with the noun that fits logically. (You may want to consult the **Vocabulaire pratique** on page 378 of your textbook.)

▷ **Jacqueline veut faire du thé. Elle met de l'eau dans** _une casserole_ .

1. Marcel veut faire une omelette. Il met les œufs dans _____ .

2. Henri veut faire du feu. Il cherche _____ et _____ .

3. Paul et André veulent dormir. Ils vont sous _____ .

4. Oh là là, il fait froid la nuit! Je prends _____ .

5. Nous partons. Nous mettons nos provisions (*food*) dans _____ .

6. Christine veut regarder l'horizon. Elle prend _____ .

A1. GUIDE À PARIS

Marie-France is showing some Canadian friends around Paris. They keep asking which place they will visit next. Fill in the *interrogative pronouns* they are using.

Marie-France:	les amis:
▷ **Nous allons visiter un musée.**	_Lequel ?_
1. Nous visiterons une église.	_____
2. Nous visiterons des magasins.	_____
3. Nous passerons devant une université.	_____
4. Nous nous promènerons dans un parc.	_____
5. Nous verrons des monuments anciens.	_____
6. Nous passerons devant des vieilles maisons.	_____

B1. SHOPPING

When he goes shopping, Philippe knows exactly what he wants to buy. Complete his answers.
(Use **désirer** and a form of **celui-ci** when his answer is **oui**. Use **préférer** and a form of **celui-là** when his answer is **non**.)

le vendeur:	Philippe:
▷ **Voulez-vous ce sac?**	Oui, _je désire celui-ci_ .
▷ **Et cette montre?**	Non, _je préfère celle-là_ .
1. Et ces disques?	Oui, _____ .
2. Et ces livres?	Non, _____ .
3. Et cet appareil-photo?	Oui, _____ .
4. Et cette caméra?	Non, _____ .
5. Et ces jolies cravates?	Oui, _____ .

C1. EMPRUNTS (*Borrowed items*)

Jacques likes to borrow things. Say what he does by using the words in parentheses and the appropriate form of **celui de.**

▷ **Jacques n'a pas sa raquette. (jouer avec / son cousin)**

Il joue avec celle de son cousin.

1. Il n'a pas son appareil-photo. (prendre des photos avec / Annie)

   _____

2. Il n'a pas ses disques. (écouter / le voisin)

   _____

3. Il n'a pas son livre d'anglais. (emprunter / le professeur)

   _____

4. Il n'a pas ses jumelles. (utiliser / Marc)

   _____

5. Il n'a pas son sac de couchage. (dormir dans / sa sœur)

   _____

TRADUCTION

Give the French equivalent of each of the following sentences.

1. *You have many records. Which ones do you prefer?*

   _____

2. *I like this car but my brother prefers that one.*

   _____

3. *That's not your tent. It's Paul's.*

   _____

4. *When I do not have my camera, I borrow my mother's.*

   _____

POUR COMMUNIQUER   Camping

Imagine that you are planning a camping trip. Say which pieces of equipment you have and from whom you are going to borrow those you do not have.

_____

_____

_____

_____

_____

UNITÉ 8   CAMPING

Leçon 2   Départ et arrivée

A1.   CONVERSATION

Imagine that a French girl is asking you the following questions. Answer her *affirmatively* or *negatively*, using the nouns in parentheses and the pronoun **que**, according to the model.

la jeune fille: **vous:**

⇨ **Tu aimes le football? (un sport)**   *Oui, c'est un sport que j'aime.*
                                                                       (Non, c'est un sport que je n'aime pas.)

1.   **Tu aimes Woody Allen? (un comédien)**   _____

2.   **Tu lis «Sports Illustrated»? (un magazine)**   _____

3.   **Tu regardes «60 Minutes»? (un programme)**   _____

4.   **Tu admires le président? (une personne)**   _____

5.   **Tu connais bien tes voisins? (des gens)**   _____

A2. QUI OU QUE?

Complete the following sentences with **qui** or **que.**

1. Connais-tu l'ami . . .

   _____ est sorti avec moi hier?

   _____ je vais inviter demain?

   _____ va au concert avec Paul?

   _____ parle espagnol?

2. Où as-tu mis le livre . . .

   _____ était dans ma chambre?

   _____ je t'ai prêté?

   _____ mon oncle m'a donné?

   _____ a des belles photos de Paris?

3. Vas-tu acheter la raquette . . .

   _____ coûte 200 francs?

   _____ je préfère?

   _____ Jimmy Connors recommande?

   _____ est la moins chère?

4. J'ai parlé à quelqu'un . . .

   _____ connaît ton frère.

   _____ tu ne connais pas.

   _____ j'ai trouvé très intéressant.

   _____ a visité Tahiti.

A3. EXPRESSION PERSONNELLE

Complete the following sentences with an expression of your choice.

1. Je suis une personne qui _____ .

2. L'ami idéal est une personne qui _____ .

3. J'aime être avec des gens que _____ .

4. Je suis d'accord avec les gens qui _____ .

5. J'aime regarder les programmes de télévision qui _____ .

6. J'ai des disques que _____ .

7. Mes parents ont une voiture qui _____ .

8. La France est un pays que _____ .

B1. PAS D'ACCORD!

Françoise and Nicole do not always agree. Read each of Françoise's questions, and write Nicole's answer. Use the appropriate form of **celui qui** and the words in parentheses. Study the model carefully.

▷ Françoise: **Tu préfères les garçons qui sont intellectuels?**

   Nicole: (sportifs) *Non, je préfère ceux qui sont sportifs.*

1. Françoise: Tu admires les personnes qui sont riches?

   Nicole: (sincères) _____

2. Françoise: Tu choisis la robe qui est courte?

   Nicole: (longue) _____

3. Françoise: Tu invites le garçon qui joue bien au tennis?

   Nicole: (au volley) _____

4. Françoise: Tu achètes les disques qui sont les plus chers?

   Nicole: (les moins chers) _____

B2.   AU PRÉSENT!

Pierre likes to live in the present. When Henri asks him if he liked his old acquaintances and the things he used to do, Pierre tells him that he prefers those of today. Complete Pierre's answers according to the model.

▷   **Henri:**   **Tu aimais les livres que tu lisais?**

   Pierre: **Oui, mais je préfère** *ceux que je lis maintenant* _____ .

1.   **Henri:**   **Tu aimais les disques que tu achetais?**

   Pierre: **Oui, mais je préfère** _____ .

2.   **Henri:**   **Tu aimais les amis que tu avais?**

   Pierre: **Oui, mais je préfère** _____ .

3.   **Henri:**   **Tu comprenais le professeur que tu avais?**

   Pierre: **Oui, mais je comprends mieux** _____ .

4.   **Henri:**   **Tu aimais la voiture que tu conduisais?**

   Pierre: **Oui, mais je préfère** _____ .

TRADUCTION

Give the French equivalent of each of the following sentences.

1.   *Where is the map that was on the table?*

   _____

2.   *I am inviting a girl whom you do not know.*

   _____

3.   *Do you want that magazine (over there) or the one that I am reading?*

   _____

4.   *I know this girl, but I do not know the one who is speaking to Paul.*

   _____

   _____

POUR COMMUNIQUER Une carte

Prepare a map of the area around your city. Indicate the compass points, the highways, and the distances (in kilometers) between the main places of interest.

UNITÉ 8 CAMPING

Leçon 3 Dispute et réconciliation

V1. À LA CAMPAGNE

The following people are spending the weekend in the country. Say what things or animals they may see there. Use the verb **voir**. (If necessary, you may want to consult the **Vocabulaire pratique** on page 389 of your textbook.)

▷ **Janine est près d'un lac.**

Elle voit des poissons (des canards...).

1. Albert est à la ferme (*farm*) de son oncle.

2. Nous sommes dans une forêt.

3. Vous êtes dans une prairie.

4. Je suis dans un parc.

A1. POURQUOI?

Explain why people do the following things. For each sentence use the appropriate form of the verb in parentheses and the *infinitive*.

▷ **Albert travaille. (devoir)**

Il doit travailler.

1. Jacqueline prend des photos. (aimer)

2. Antoine sort avec nous. (pouvoir)

3. Paul ski. (savoir)

4. Sylvie va au cinéma. (vouloir)

5. Hélène fait du camping. (avoir envie de)

6. Béatrice se repose. (avoir besoin de)

A2. IL PLEUT!

It's raining hard now. Read what the following people usually do on weekends. Say that they prefer not to do these things today. Use the construction **préférer** + *negative* infinitive.

d'habitude: ce week-end:

▷ **Nous sortons.** *Nous préférons ne pas sortir.*

1. Denis joue au tennis. _____

2. Je fais du camping. _____

3. Vous allez à la campagne. _____

4. Tu prends des photos. _____

5. Nous faisons un pique-nique. _____

B1. LE CLUB DE TENNIS

Several students have registered for a tennis course, but they are not all good players. Describe each one by completing the sentences below with **à** or **de,** as appropriate.

1. Guillaume a décidé _____ prendre des leçons.

2. Martine apprend _____ servir.

3. Charles commence _____ jouer assez bien.

4. Thomas rêve _____ être un grand champion.

5. Philippe accepte _____ jouer avec lui.

6. Sylvie refuse _____ jouer avec Thomas.

7. Charlotte hésite _____ participer au championnat (*championship tournament*).

8. Thérèse continue _____ faire des progrès.

9. Paul essaie _____ gagner son match.

10. Jacqueline a fini _____ jouer.

B2.   **UNE FILLE PARFAITE** (*A perfect girl*)

Michèle is a perfect girl. Express this by using the verbs in parentheses in the construction
verb + infinitive. Your sentences may be *affirmative* or *negative*.

▷   **Michèle aide ses amis? (hésiter?)**

Elle n' hésite pas à aider ses amis.

1.   Elle prête ses disques? (accepter?)

   _____

2.   Elle dit des mensonges? (refuser?)

   _____

3.   Elle est de bonne humeur? (cesser?)

   _____

4.   Elle écrit à ses grands-parents? (oublier?)

   _____

5.   Elle est impartiale? (essayer?)

   _____

6.   Elle est généreuse? (continuer?)

   _____

TRADUCTION

Give the French equivalent of each of the following sentences.

1.   *I am learning to drive.*

   _____

2.   *Why do you hesitate to answer?*

   _____

3.   *Béatrice has agreed to have dinner with us.*

   _____

4.   *Philippe dreams of driving a Jaguar.*

   _____

POUR COMMUNIQUER Vos projets

Talk about yourself and your plans. Complete each of the sentences below with a personal expression.

J'apprends _____ .

Je voudrais apprendre _____ .

J'essaie _____ .

J'ai décidé _____ .

Je rêve _____ .

UNITÉ 8   CAMPING

Leçon 4   Une nuit agitée

V1.   LE CIEL

What we see in the sky depends on the time of day and on the weather. Complete each of the following sentences with the appropriate noun. (You may want to consult the **Vocabulaire pratique** on pages 396–397 of your textbook.)

1.   Le matin on peut voir _____ à l'est.

2.   Quand il fait nuit, on peut voir _____ et _____ .

3.   Quand il pleut, il y a _____ dans le ciel.

4.   Quand il y a un orage, on peut voir _____ .

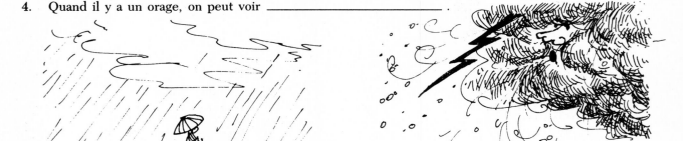

A1.   L'ORDRE LOGIQUE

In general we have to do certain things before doing others. Express this by deciding which of the two actions in parentheses comes first. Study the model carefully.

▷   **(se coucher / se déshabiller)**

    Nous *nous déshabillons avant de nous coucher* .

1.   (faire les courses / prendre de l'argent)

    Ma mère _____ .

2.   (payer / sortir du restaurant)

    Vous _____ .

3.   (se marier / se fiancer)

    Paul et Valérie _____ .

4.   (acheter les billets / aller au théâtre)

    J'_____ .

5.   (sortir / s'habiller)

    Tu _____ .

A2. OUBLIS! (*Oversights*)

Monsieur Jean Delalune celebrated his birthday until late into the night. The next morning he was so tired he went to work without doing the following things. Describe what happened.

CE MATIN: Il ne se rase pas. Il ne déjeune pas. Il n'écoute pas la radio. Il ne dit pas au revoir à sa femme. Il ne prend pas son manteau. Il ne prend pas d'argent.

Il est parti sans *se raser, sans* _____

_____

_____

A3. LE CONTRAIRE (*The opposite*)

The following people are doing the opposite of what they are supposed to do. Express this according to the model.

▷ (dormir) **Philippe ne travaille pas.**

Il dort au lieu de travailler. _____

1. (s'amuser) Les élèves n'étudient pas.

_____

2. (regarder la télé) Mon petit frère ne dort pas.

_____

3. (jouer au volley) Tu n'aides pas ta mère.

_____

4. (aller au cinéma) Vous ne préparez pas l'examen.

_____

5. (grossir) André ne maigrit pas.

_____

A4. OBJECTIFS PROFESSIONNELS (*Professional goals*)

Different people have different reasons to choose their professions. Explain the choices of the people below by using elements from columns A and B in logical sentences.

A	B
médecin	voyager
avocat	gagner de l'argent
journaliste	aider les autres (*other people*)
professeur	avoir beaucoup de vacances
pilote	rencontrer des personnes intéressantes
infirmier/infirmière	
guide touristique	

➡ André *veut être guide touristique pour voyager* .

1. Je _____ .

2. Vous _____ .

3. Nous _____ .

4. Mes cousins _____ .

5. Éric _____ .

6. Tu _____ .

TRADUCTION

Give the French equivalent of each of the following sentences.

1. *Jeanne left without saying good-by.*

   _____

2. *Call me before going to the movies.*

   _____

3. *Instead of inviting Claire, I invited Martine.*

   _____

4. *Jean-Louis wants to buy a car to go to Québec.*

   _____

POUR COMMUNIQUER   Études universitaires (*University studies*)

Ask five friends who are going to go to college why they want to go. Then report the results of your survey.

▷ *Paul veut aller à l'université pour étudier la biologie.*

_____

_____

_____

_____

_____

_____

_____

_____

UNITÉ 8   CAMPING
Leçon 5   Les manœuvres

A1.   LA JOURNÉE DE GEORGES

When he described the events of the day, Georges forgot to mention the "hows" and the "whens." Help him by filling in the blanks with the *present participle* of the verb in parentheses.

▷   (regarder)   J'ai déjeuné en _regardant_ la télé.

1.   (aller)   J'ai rencontré Jacques en _____ à la poste.

2.   (attendre)   J'ai parlé à Denise en _____ le bus.

3.   (rentrer)   J'ai vu un accident en _____ à la maison.

4.   (lire)   Je me suis reposé en _____ un roman policier.

5.   (finir)   J'ai compris le mystère en _____ le livre.

A2.B1.   MÉTHODE DIRECTE

According to many people, you can only learn something by doing it. Complete each of the sentences below by adding **en** + *present participle*, according to the model.

▷   **Tu apprendras à danser** _en dansant_ .

1.   Vous apprendrez à chanter _____ .

2.   Colette apprendra à faire du ski _____ .

3.   Gérard apprendra à conduire _____ .

4.   Hubert apprendra à jouer de la guitare _____ .

5.   Ils apprendront à obéir _____ .

B2.   CHACUN A SA MÉTHODE. (*Everyone has his own method.*)

The following people are learning a foreign language. Say which language each one is learning and describe the method used, according to the model: **l'allemand / l'anglais / l'espagnol / le français.**

▷   **Ma cousine écoute Radio-France.**

   Elle apprend le français en écoutant Radio-France.

1.   Paul et Denis écoutent Radio-Montréal.

   _____

2.   Antoine sort avec une Américaine.

   _____

3.   Nous sortons avec des amis allemands.

   _____

4.   Je lis des journaux mexicains.

   _____

5.   Vous parlez avec vos amis espagnols.

   _____

C1. UNE QUESTION DE STYLE (A matter of style)

Imagine that you are an editor for a French magazine. You have decided to change the following expressions by using verbal adjectives in **—ant.** Follow the model, making the agreement where necessary.

▷   des filles qui amusent   *des filles amusantes*

1. une histoire qui amuse   _____
2. des élèves qui obéissent   _____
3. un chien qui obéit   _____
4. un climat qui change   _____
5. une attitude qui change   _____
6. un couteau qui coupe   _____

TRADUCTION

Give the French equivalent of each of the following sentences.

1. *I listen to the radio while studying.*

   _____

2. *You will earn money by working.*

   _____

3. *I met Philippe while going to the restaurant.*

   _____

4. *Upon arriving, I phoned Michèle.*

   _____

POUR COMMUNIQUER   Occupations de week-end (Weekend activities)

Ask four friends how they keep busy during the weekend. Then report on each one's activities, according to the model. (Note: **s'occuper** = *to keep busy*)

▷   *Charles s'occupe en jouant au tennis et en regardant la télé.*

_____

_____

_____

_____

_____

Récréation culturelle

La France en auto

Imaginez que vous faites un voyage en Europe avec votre famille. Vous allez passer six jours en France. Vous arrivez à Paris et vous décidez de louer une voiture. Regardez la liste des voitures que vous pouvez louer et les prix.

Applicable au 5 Avril / Valid as of April 5			PLACES/SEATS	PORTES/DOORS	RADIO/RADIO	CASSETTE/CASSETTE	AIR CONDITIONNE/AIR CONDITIONNED	GRAND COFFRE/LARGE TRUNK	TARIFS/RATES	
CATEGORIES		MODELES / MODELS (1)							PAR JOUR F.F. / PER DAY F.F.	PAR KM F.F. / PER KM F.F.
ECONOMIQUE / SUB COMPACT	A	FORD FIESTA SUPER FESTIVAL / RENAULT SUPER 5 FIVE / PEUGEOT 205 JUNIOR / UNO 45 FIRE / OPEL CORSA GL	4	2	X				211,20	2,69
	B	RENAULT SUPER 5 SL / PEUGEOT 205 GL	4	4	X				220,16	3,14
MOYENNE / MEDIUM SIZE	C	FORD ESCORT 1,6 CL / OPEL KADETT 1200 / PEUGEOT 309 GL PROFIL / RENAULT 11 GTL	5	4	X				254,72	3,72
	D	FORD SIERRA 1800 CL / PEUGEOT 405 GR / RENAULT 21 GTS / BMW 316	5	4	X	X		X	343,04	4,83
SUPERIEURE / FULL SIZE	E	FORD SCORPIO 2.0 GLI "ABS" / RENAULT 25 GTS / OPEL OMEGA 2.0 I GL	5	4	X	X		X	394,24	5,08

1. Quelle voiture choisissez-vous? Pourquoi?

_____

Pendant six jours de votre voyage, vous décidez de visiter les cinq villes et les cinq provinces suivantes:

> Rouen (en Normandie)   Nîmes (en Provence)
> Tours (en Touraine)   Biarritz (au Pays Basque)
> Strasbourg (en Alsace)

2. Mettez ces villes et ces provinces sur la carte de France.

3. Préparez un itinéraire jour par jour en indiquant le nom des villes où vous vous arrêterez chaque nuit. Pour chaque jour, indiquez le nombre approximatif de kilomètres. Consultez un atlas.

4. Indiquez votre itinéraire sur la carte.

	DÉPART	ARRIVÉE	KILOMÈTRES
1er jour	*Paris*		
2e jour			
3e jour			
4e jour			
5e jour			
6e jour			

Unité 8

Récréation culturelle

Choisissez une ville ou une région que vous visitez et faites la description de cette ville ou de cette région (histoire, monuments, choses à visiter ou à voir, spécialités régionales, industries, etc.). (Source: encyclopédie, almanach, brochures touristiques, etc.)

_____

_____

_____

_____

_____

C'est la fin de votre voyage en France. Préparez votre note de location (*rental bill*) de voiture. Remplissez la fiche (*card*) suivante.

LOCATION DE VOITURE

jour	kilomètres
1	
2	
3	
4	
5	
6	

nombre de kilomètres ☐ × prix/kilomètre ☐ = ☐

nombre de jours ☐ × prix/jour ☐ = ☐

TOTAL: = ☐

Récréation culturelle

Camping au Canada

Avec ses forêts, ses lacs, ses plages, ses parcs, le Canada est un endroit idéal pour passer les vacances. La région au nord-est de Québec est particulièrement pittoresque. C'est dans cette région qu'est situé le camping «Le Génévrier».

Lisez attentivement la brochure.

LE **GENEVRIER** INC.
camping plage

Baie St-Paul, Cté Charlevoix, P.Q., Rte 138, 60 milles de Québec
Téléphone: 435-6520

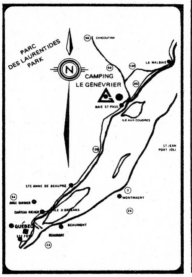

GLOSSAIRE: **pédalo** *pedal boat* **plongeon** *diving* **glissoire** *slide*
équitation *horseback riding* **balle molle** *softball*

Imaginez que vous passez quelques jours dans ce camping. Écrivez une carte postale à un(e) ami(e) où vous décrivez le camping et où vous parlez de vos activités.

QUÉBEC — CANADA

Distributeur Emile Kirouac Enr., 228 - 7e Rue, Québec, Canada

post card - carte postale

Récréation culturelle

Vous avez la parole: Une semaine à la campagne

Monsieur Tardieu habite dans une grande ville. Il décide de passer une semaine à la campagne. Regardez la bande dessinée et décrivez jour par jour la semaine de Monsieur Tardieu.

Samedi, _____

_____

_____

_____

_____

Dimanche, _____

_____

_____

_____

_____

VOCABULAIRE: **un coq** *rooster*
réveiller *to wake up*

Lundi, _____

_____

_____

_____

_____

VOCABULAIRE: **un taureau** *bull*
attaquer *to attack*

Mardi, _____

_____

_____

_____

_____

VOCABULAIRE: **une fourmi** *ant*

Mercredi, _____

_____

_____

_____

_____

VOCABULAIRE:
un moustique *mosquito*
piquer *to sting* **tuer** *to kill*

Jeudi, _____

_____

_____

_____

_____

VOCABULAIRE: **une oie** *goose*

Vendredi, _____

_____

_____

_____

_____

Samedi, _____

_____

_____

_____

_____

TESTS DE CONTRÔLE ▪ REPRISE
Verbes

TEST 1   OUI ET NON

Say what the people on the left do, using the appropriate forms of the verbs in parentheses. Then say that their friends on the right do *not* do the same things.

▷   (jouer)   Pierre *joue* _____ au tennis.   Tu *ne joues pas au tennis* .

1.   (danser)   Catherine _____ .   Ses amies _____ .

2.   (travailler) Je _____ .   Vous _____ .

3.   (maigrir)   Je _____ .   Mes amis _____ .

4.   (obéir)   Vous _____ .   Henri _____ .

5.   (réussir)   Nous _____ à l'examen.   Vous _____ .

6.   (attendre)   Les élèves _____   Tu _____ .
                   le professeur.

7.   (répondre)   Vous _____ .   Je _____ .

TEST 2   S'IL VOUS PLAÎT!

Tell the people mentioned below to do the first thing in parentheses and *not* to do the second. Use the appropriate forms of the *imperative* of the suggested verbs. (Note: Use the **tu** form in sentences 1 and 2, and the **vous** form in sentences 3, 4, and 5.)

1.   Jacqueline (téléphoner / répondre)

     _____ à Philippe! _____ à Sylvie!

2.   Thomas (travailler / perdre)

     _____ ! _____ ton temps!

3.   Paul et Antoine (maigrir / grossir)

     _____ ! _____ !

4.   Madame Durand (jouer / vendre)

     _____ au tennis! _____ votre raquette!

5.   Claire et Stéphanie (être / être)

     _____ patientes! _____ impatientes!

TEST 3 CATHERINE ET SES AMIS

Complete the descriptions of Catherine and her friends. Fill in the blanks of each description with the appropriate forms of the verbs **être, avoir,** and **aller,** in that order.

1. Catherine _____ une championne de tennis. Elle _____ une très bonne

   raquette. Elle _____ jouer avec nous demain.

2. Paul et Henri _____ musiciens. Ils _____ une guitare et un banjo.

   Ils _____ souvent au concert avec Catherine.

3. Nous _____ américains. Nous _____ des amis en France.

   Nous _____ visiter Paris avec eux.

4. Vous _____ des élèves intelligents. Vous _____ des professeurs sympathiques.

   Vous _____ à la bibliothèque cet après-midi.

TEST 4 QUESTIONS ET RÉPONSES

Read the following answers on the right, paying attention to the information they contain. Then formulate the corresponding questions, using the subjects and the verbs in parentheses. In your questions use **est-ce que** and, if necessary, the required question words.

questions: **réponses:**

1. (tu / habiter?)

   _____ ?   À Montréal.

2. (vous / parler français?)

   _____ ?   Oui.

3. (Jacques / voyager?)

   _____ ?   En autobus.

4. (tes amis / écouter?)

   _____ ?   Un concert de jazz.

5. (tu / téléphoner?)

   _____ ?   À mon cousin.

6. (Charles / habiter à Québec?)

   _____ ?   Non.

Structure

TEST 5 QU'EST-CE QU'ILS ONT?

Describe what the following people have, using the nouns in parentheses and the appropriate forms of the adjectives in italics. Be sure to put each adjective in its proper position.

⇨ **Philippe est *sympathique*. (des amis)** **Il a** _des amis sympathiques_ .

1. Georges est *intéressant*. (des cousines) Il a _____ .
2. Albert est *petit*. (une voiture) Il a _____ .
3. Sylvie est *jolie*. (des robes) Elle a _____ .
4. Christine est *anglaise*. (des amies) Elle a _____ .
5. Paul et Marc sont *français*. (des disques) Ils ont _____ .

TEST 6 QU'EST-CE QU'ILS FONT?

Describe what the following people are doing, using the elements below in complete sentences.

⇨ **Jacques / parler à / l'étudiante**

Il _parle à l'étudiante_ .

1. le professeur / parler à / les élèves

   Il _____ .
2. nous / aller à / la piscine

   Nous _____ .
3. vous / jouer à / le tennis

   Vous _____ .
4. nous / rentrer de / la plage

   Nous _____ .
5. Marthe / jouer de / le piano

   Elle _____ .
6. nous / parler à / les frères de / les garçons français

   Nous _____ .

TEST 7 DESCRIPTIONS

Describe the people and objects in parentheses. Complete the sentences below with **Il/Elle est** or **C'est,** as appropriate.

1. (Jacqueline) _____ la sœur de Paul. _____ grande et blonde.
2. (Robert) _____ brun. _____ un garçon amusant.
3. (la moto de Robert) _____ japonaise. _____ une Kawasaki.
4. (le sac de Sophie) _____ un sac français. _____ très joli.

TEST 8 QUI?

Rewrite each of the sentences below, replacing the noun(s) in italics with the appropriate *subject* or *stress* pronoun(s).

▷ *Philippe* est avec *Suzanne.* ___Il___ est avec ___elle___ .

1. C'est *Élisabeth!* C'est _____ !

2. Ce n'est pas *Monsieur Durand!* Ce n'est pas _____ !

3. Est-ce qu'*Hélène* est chez *Henri?* Est-ce qu'_____ est chez _____ ?

4. Est-ce qu'*Antoine* voyage avec *ses cousins?* Est-ce qu'_____ voyage avec _____ ?

5. *Paul* va au théâtre avec *Isabelle et Caroline.* _____ va au théâtre avec _____ .

6. *Christine* et *Georges* sont des amis sympathiques. _____ et _____ sont des amis sympathiques.

TEST 9 EN FAMILLE

The following people do certain things for or with members of their families or their friends. Express this by filling in each blank with the appropriate *possessive adjective* that corresponds to the *subject* of the sentence.

▷ Je visite Paris avec ___mes___ cousins.

1. Nous voyageons avec _____ cousines et _____ oncle.

2. Vincent va au cinéma avec _____ sœur et _____ frère.

3. Isabelle est à la plage avec _____ ami Simon et _____ amie Denise.

4. Jacques et Henri jouent au tennis avec _____ cousins.

5. Est-ce que vous allez inviter _____ professeur et _____ camarades de classe?

TEST 10 GÉOGRAPHIE

Rewrite each of the sentences below by replacing the name of the *city* with the name of the *country* in which it is located. Make all necessary changes.

▷ **Robert habite à Paris.** Il habite ___en France___ .

1. Nous sommes à Québec. Nous sommes _____ .

2. Suzanne aime New York. Elle aime _____ .

3. Isabelle rentre de Berlin. Elle rentre _____ .

4. Je visite Mexico. Je visite _____ .

5. Nous allons à Chicago. Nous allons _____ .

6. Tu habites à Madrid. Tu habites _____ .

TEST 11 EN FRANÇAIS

Complete the French equivalent of each of the following sentences.

1. *I have a cassette recorder but I don't have any cassettes.*

   J'ai un magnétophone mais je _____ .

2. *Suzanne has no friends in Paris.*

   Suzanne _____ à Paris.

3. *Christine loves sports. She likes tennis a lot.*

   Christine aime _____ . Elle aime beaucoup _____ .

4. *I am not having supper at home tonight.*

   Je ne dîne pas _____ ce soir.

5. *Nathalie is going to Éric's house.*

   Nathalie va _____ .

6. *Robert is going to play tennis but we are not going to play with him.*

   Robert _____ au tennis mais nous _____ avec lui.

7. *Do you have Pierre's records?*

   Est-ce que tu as _____ ?

8. *Where is Marie's sister?*

   Où est _____ ?

Vocabulaire

TEST 12 ACTIVITÉS

Say what the following people are doing. Complete each sentence with the French equivalent of the expression in parentheses.

▷ (speaks to) Pierre *parle à* _____ Jeannette.

1. (*looks at*) Charles _____ Christine.
2. (*listens to*) Suzanne _____ ses disques.
3. (*phones*) Élisabeth _____ Jacques.
4. (*works*) Robert _____ avec nous.
5. (*obeys*) Claude _____ son père.
6. (*waits for*) Gisèle _____ Claire.
7. (*visits*) Nathalie _____ son oncle.
8. (*answers*) Albert _____ Charlotte.

TEST 13   LEURS POSSESSIONS (*Their belongings*)

Describe what the following people own by completing the sentences with the nouns suggested by the illustrations. Use the appropriate *indefinite articles*.

1. Jacques a _____ et _____ .

2. Sylvie a _____ et _____ .

3. Antoine a _____ et _____ .

4. Suzanne a _____ et _____ .

5. Monsieur Masson a _____ et _____ .

TEST 14   AVANT ET APRÈS

Write the numbers, days, months, seasons, or dates which come *before* and *after* the following:

avant (*before*):		après (*after*):
⇨ _deux_	trois	_quatre_
1. _____	dix	_____
2. _____	seize	_____
3. _____	vingt	_____
4. _____	quatre-vingts	_____
5. _____	lundi	_____
6. _____	jeudi	_____
7. _____	février	_____
8. _____	juillet	_____
9. _____	automne	_____
10. _____	le deux décembre	_____

TESTS DE CONTRÔLE ▪ UNITÉ 1
Verbes

TEST 1 WEEK-END

Explain the weekend plans of the people below. Fill in the blanks with the appropriate forms of the *present* tense of the verbs in parentheses.

1. (vouloir) Jacques _____ sortir avec Suzanne. Pierre et André _____

   aller au cinéma. Nous _____ faire un pique-nique. Et toi, qu'est-ce que

   tu _____ faire?

2. (devoir) Nous _____ aller chez nos amis. Je _____ rendre visite à

   Claire. Mes cousins _____ étudier. Et vous, qu'est-ce que

   vous _____ faire?

3. (pouvoir) Alain et Georges ne _____ pas sortir dimanche. Je _____

   sortir samedi soir. Nous _____ aller à un concert. Est-ce que

   vous _____ venir avec nous?

TEST 2 QU'EST-CE QU'ILS FONT?

Describe what the following people are doing. Fill in the blanks with the appropriate forms of the *present* tense of the verbs in parentheses.

1. (faire) Aujourd'hui, nous _____ une promenade à la campagne. Julien

   _____ un pique-nique. André et sa sœur _____

   du camping. Et vous, qu'est-ce que vous _____ ?

2. (venir) Mes amis _____ chez moi ce soir. Henri _____

   avec sa sœur. Et vous, avec qui est-ce que vous _____ ?

3. (sortir) Nous _____ souvent. Je _____ avec Caroline.

   Mes cousins _____ avec leurs amies américaines. Et toi, est-ce que

   tu _____ ce soir?

4. (prendre) Nous _____ notre voiture. Hélène _____

   son vélo. Albert et Charles _____ leur moto. Est-ce que

   tu _____ ta moto aussi?

5. (conduire) Richard et Suzanne _____ souvent la voiture de leurs parents.

   Suzanne _____ très bien. Et vous, comment _____ -vous?

6. (mettre) Je _____ mon short. Nathalie et Julie _____

   leurs blue-jeans. Quels vêtements est-ce que vous _____ ?

7. (boire) Nous _____ du jus de fruit. Je _____ du jus

   d'orange. Caroline et Thomas _____ du jus de tomate. Et vous,

   qu'est-ce que vous _____ ?

TEST 3　HIER

Yesterday the people below did the first thing in parentheses but *not* the second. Express this by filling in the blanks with the appropriate *affirmative* and *negative* forms of the **passé composé** of the suggested verbs.

1. (étudier / regarder)　Nous _____ .

   Nous _____ la télé.

2. (travailler / perdre)　Jacques _____ .

   Il _____ son temps.

3. (acheter / choisir)　Mes cousins _____ ces pulls noirs.

   Ils _____ ces pulls rouges.

4. (écouter / finir)　Vous _____ vos disques.

   Vous _____ ce livre.

5. (rendre / attendre)　Tu _____ visite à ton oncle.

   Tu _____ tes amis.

6. (vendre / acheter)　J'_____ mon walkman.

   Je _____ des nouvelles cassettes.

7. (choisir / dépenser)　Élisabeth _____ une nouvelle robe.

   Elle _____ beaucoup d'argent.

8. (jouer / gagner)　Robert et Paul _____ au tennis.

   Ils _____ .

TEST 4　L'ÉTÉ DERNIER

Describe what the people below did last summer by filling in each blank with the appropriate **passé composé** form of the verb in parentheses.

1. (faire)　Ma sœur _____ un voyage au Mexique.

2. (être)　Robert _____ invité par (*by*) un ami français.

3. (avoir)　Philippe _____ un accident de moto.

4. (apprendre)　Thérèse _____ à faire du ski nautique.

5. (conduire)　Albert _____ la Jaguar de son cousin.

6. (boire)　Monsieur Roland _____ du champagne pour son anniversaire.

7. (mettre)　Gisèle _____ son nouveau maillot de bain.

8. (vouloir)　Sylvie _____ faire de la planche à voile.

9. (devoir)　Thomas _____ travailler.

10. (pouvoir)　Jean-Jacques _____ acheter une caméra.

TEST 5   OÙ SONT-ILS ALLÉS?

Say where the following people went yesterday and what they did. Fill in the first blank of each item with the appropriate **passé composé** form of **aller.** Fill in the second blank with the appropriate **passé composé** form of the verb in parentheses. Be careful! Some of these verbs are conjugated with **avoir** and others with **être.**

1. Hélène _____ au cinéma.

    Elle _____ avec Paul. (sortir)

2. Charles _____ au supermarché.

    Il _____ de la limonade. (acheter)

3. Philippe et Alain _____ à un concert.

    Ils _____ à minuit. (rentrer)

4. Sylvie et Lucie _____ au café.

    Elles _____ là-bas deux heures avec des amis. (rester)

5. Paul et moi, nous _____ à la plage.

    Nous _____ . (nager)

6. Luc et toi, vous _____ chez Louise.

    Vous _____ chez vous à neuf heures. (revenir)

Structure

TEST 6   AU RESTAURANT

The people below are at a restaurant that offers the dishes mentioned in parentheses. Explain what everyone does by completing the sentences. Use the appropriate *partitive articles*.

1. (le rosbif)   Philippe commande _____ .
2. (le caviar)   Non, Robert ne prend pas _____ .
3. (les spaghetti) Christine mange _____ .
4. (les œufs)   Non, Charlotte ne mange pas _____ .
5. (la salade)   Suzanne prend _____ .
6. (la glace)   Non, Thérèse ne mange pas _____ .

TEST 7   ARTICLE PARTITIF OU ARTICLE DÉFINI?

Note the *gender* (masculine or feminine) and *number* (singular or plural) of the nouns in parentheses. Then complete the sentences with the appropriate *partitive* or *definite* articles.

1. (la viande)   Catherine déteste _____ viande.
2. (le rosbif)   Nous mangeons souvent _____ rosbif.
3. (les œufs)   Est-ce qu'il y a _____ œufs dans le réfrigérateur?
4. (le lait)   _____ lait est sur la table.
5. (le sucre)   Prenez-vous _____ sucre avec votre café?

6. (l'argent)   Un millionnaire est une personne qui a _____ argent.

7. (l'ambition)   Ma sœur a _____ ambition.

8. (la patience) _____ patience est une vertu (*virtue*).

TEST 8   EN FRANÇAIS

Complete the French equivalent of each of the following sentences.

1. *In Quebec City, people speak French.*

   À Québec, _____ français.

2. *When one is young, one likes music.*

   Quand _____ jeune, _____ la musique.

3. *My uncle is an architect.*

   Mon oncle _____ .

4. *Caroline wants to be a teacher.*

   Caroline veut _____ .

5. *In order to drive, one must be eighteen.*

   Pour conduire, _____ avoir 18 ans.

6. *To go to France, you have to have a passport.*

   Pour aller en France, _____ avoir un passeport.

7. *Pierre is putting on his sweater because he is cold.*

   Pierre met son pull parce qu'il _____ .

8. *I insist when I am right.*

   J'insiste quand j'_____ .

9. *Did Hélène speak to Jean-Paul?*

   _____ à Jean-Paul?

10. *Did they play golf yesterday?*

    _____ au golf hier?

11. *I have just spoken to Antoine.*

    _____ à Antoine.

12. *My cousins have just bought a sports car.*

    Mes cousins _____ une voiture de sport.

Vocabulaire

TEST 9 L'INTRUS (*The intruder*)

The following sentences can be logically completed by two of the three suggested verbs. The verb that *does not* fit is the intruder. Circle it.

1. Henri _____ de la salade.   boit   commande   veut
2. Christine _____ de la limonade.   mange   boit   prend
3. Mon père _____ une Cadillac.   conduit   loue   traduit
4. Gilles _____ l'italien.   prend   apprend   comprend
5. Jacques _____ de l'argent.   gagne   dépense   dure
6. Isabelle _____ une robe.   met   permet   achète
7. Éric _____ à huit heures.   part   sort   met
8. Sylvie _____ à l'hôtel.   reste   va   tombe

TEST 10 LES AMIS DE SIMONE

Read about Simone's friends. Then complete each sentence with an expression with **faire** (items 1–4) or **avoir** (items 5–8). Be logical!

1. Caroline est au supermarché. Elle _____ .
2. Roland est à Québec. Il _____ au Canada.
3. Thomas est à la campagne. Il _____ à bicyclette.
4. Suzanne prépare le dîner. Elle aime _____ .
5. Albert veut dormir. Il _____ .
6. Christine boit du Coca-Cola. Elle _____ .
7. Gilbert ôte (*takes off*) son pull. Il _____ .
8. Charlotte veut aller à la discothèque. Elle _____ de danser.

TEST 11 CATÉGORIES

Give two items that fit each of the following categories. Use the appropriate articles.

▷ (2 **sports**)   *le tennis, le football* _____

1. (2 **kinds of meat**) _____

2. (2 **kinds of fish**) _____

3. (2 **vegetables**) _____

4. (2 **fruits**) _____

5. (2 **dairy products**) _____

6. (2 **meals**) _____

7. (2 **non-alcoholic beverages**) _____

8. (2 **alcoholic beverages**) _____

9. (2 **water sports**) _____

10. (2 **winter sports**) _____

TESTS DE CONTRÔLE ▪ UNITÉ 2
Verbes

TEST 1   QU'EST-CE QU'ILS FONT?

Complete the following sentences with the appropriate forms of the *present tense* of the verbs in parentheses.

1. (lire)   Je _____ un livre mais mes amis _____ des bandes

    dessinées. Et toi, qu'est-ce que tu _____ ?

2. (écrire)   Nous _____ à nos amis. J'_____ à Caroline. Pierre et

    Denis _____ à leurs amies.

3. (dire)   Est-ce que vous _____ la vérité? Moi, je _____ toujours

    ce que (*what*) je pense, mais mes cousins _____ souvent des mensonges.

4. (voir)   Olivier _____ Thérèse. Marthe et Irène _____ leurs

    amis français. Et vous, qui _____-vous ce week-end?

5. (connaître)   Est-ce que tes amis _____ mon frère? Est-ce que vous _____

    Sylvie? Est-ce qu'André _____ Anne?

6. (savoir)   Je _____ que vous _____ la vérité. Est-ce que

    vos amis _____ la vérité aussi?

TEST 2   HIER

Say what the following people did yesterday by completing each of the sentences below with the appropriate **passé composé** form of the verb in parentheses.

1. (lire)   Philippe _____ un magazine anglais.

2. (écrire)   Nathalie _____ à sa tante.

3. (dire)   Albert _____ quelque chose d'amusant à ses amis.

4. (voir)   Suzanne _____ un film d'horreur.

5. (reconnaître)   Isabelle _____ son professeur d'histoire dans la rue (*street*).

6. (savoir)   Marc _____ qui a pris sa raquette.

Unité deux   **201**

Structure

TEST 3 JACQUELINE

Complete the descriptions of Jacqueline's activities by filling in the blanks with the appropriate forms of the adjectives in parentheses. Pay attention to the *gender* and *number* of the corresponding nouns.

1. (nouveau) Jacqueline va dans un magasin. Là, elle achète une _____ calculatrice,

   un _____ appareil-photo, des _____ disques français et

   des _____ cassettes anglaises.

2. (vieux) Jacqueline va à la campagne. Elle met ses _____ bottes noires,

   son _____ anorak bleu et une _____ chemise.

3. (beau) Jacqueline va à une boum. Elle met une _____ robe,

   ses _____ chaussures blanches, un _____ collier et

   trois _____ bracelets indiens.

TEST 4 RESSEMBLANCE (*Similarity*)

The following people have friends with personalities similar to their own. Complete each sentence with the appropriate form of the adjective in italics.

1. Robert est *original*. Pierre et Paul sont _____ aussi.

2. Thomas est *loyal*. Nicole et Monique sont _____ aussi.

3. Albert est *curieux*. Élisabeth est _____ aussi.

4. André est *généreux*. Ses amis sont _____ aussi.

5. Roland est *sportif*. Béatrice est _____ aussi.

6. Jean-Michel est *musicien*. Isabelle et Caroline sont _____ aussi.

7. Bernard est *ponctuel*. Irène est _____ aussi.

8. Éric est *mignon*. Stéphanie est _____ aussi.

TEST 5   ENTRE AMIS

Rewrite each of the following sentences, using a *direct object pronoun* to replace the word(s) in italics. (Be careful with the agreement of the past participle in sentences 9–12.)

▷   Paul regarde *Antoine*.   Paul *le regarde* .

1.   Pierre invite *Béatrice*.   Pierre _____ .

2.   Danièle connaît *ces garçons*.   Danièle _____ .

3.   Je ne connais pas *Georges*.   Je _____ .

4.   Nous trouvons *ta cousine* sympathique.   Nous _____ sympathique.

5.   Invite *Suzanne*!   _____ !

6.   N'invitons pas *ces filles*!   _____ !

7.   Je vais aider *Jacqueline*.   Je vais _____ .

8.   Nous n'allons pas voir *nos cousins*.   Nous n'allons pas _____ .

9.   Charles a vu *Christine*.   Charles _____ .

10.   Jean n'a pas aidé *Marc*.   Jean _____ .

11.   Tu as rencontré *mes amis*.   Tu _____ .

12.   Vous n'avez pas vu *mes sœurs*.   Vous _____ .

TEST 6   LES AMIS DE MARC

Describe what Marc does for his family and friends. Complete the sentences below with the appropriate *direct* or *indirect* object pronouns that correspond to the people mentioned in parentheses.

1.   (Catherine)   Marc _____ téléphone souvent.

2.   (Jean-Paul)   Il _____ parle de ses projets.

3.   (Raymond et Éric)   Il _____ invite chez lui.

4.   (Annie)   Il _____ aide.

5.   (ses cousins)   Il _____ écrit pendant les vacances.

6.   (ses sœurs)   Il _____ prête ses disques.

7.   (l'oncle Henri)   Il va _____ voir dimanche.

8.   (Suzanne)   Il va _____ donner son adresse.

TEST 7   QUI OU QUE?

Complete each of the sentences below with the relative pronoun **qui** or **que**.

1.   Marc a invité une fille _____ tu connais.

2.   Prête-moi le disque _____ est sur la table.

3.   Nous avons des amis _____ habitent à Paris.

4.   Pierre connaît les garçons _____ vous allez inviter.

5.   As-tu le livre _____ j'ai acheté hier?

6.   J'ai une amie _____ a une voiture de sport.

7.   Je n'aime pas les sports _____ sont violents.

TEST 8 EN FRANÇAIS

Complete the French equivalent of each of the following sentences.

1. *I know Marc but I don't know where he lives.*

   Je _____ Marc mais je _____ où il habite.

2. *I know how to swim.*

   Je _____ nager.

3. *Béatrice never studies on weekends.*

   Béatrice _____ le week-end.

4. *Charles has never visited the United States.*

   Charles _____ les États-Unis.

5. *Denise no longer lives in Grenoble.*

   Denise _____ à Grenoble.

6. *Sylvie is not doing anything today.*

   Sylvie _____ aujourd'hui.

7. *Philippe is not speaking to anyone.*

   Philippe _____ .

Vocabulaire

TEST 9 JACQUES ET SES AMIS

Complete each of the sentences below with the French verb that corresponds to the expression in parentheses.

1. (*finds*) Jacques _____ Annie très intelligente.

2. (*meets*) Suzanne _____ ses amis au café.

3. (*forgets*) Thomas _____ toujours la date de l'examen.

4. (*is looking for*) Jean-Claude _____ ses lunettes.

5. (*helps*) Éric _____ sa mère.

6. (*asks for*) Charles _____ l'adresse de Claire.

7. (*lends*) Marc _____ sa bicyclette à Denis.

8. (*introduces*) Oliver _____ sa cousine à ses camarades.

9. (*gives*) Jacqueline _____ son numéro de téléphone à Georges.

10. (*shows*) Gilbert _____ ses photos à Pauline.

TESTS DE CONTRÔLE • UNITÉ 3
Verbes

TEST 1 **AUJOURD'HUI**

Say what the people below are doing by completing the following sentences with the appropriate *present tense* forms of the verbs in parentheses.

1. (acheter)   Nous _____ des disques. J'_____ aussi une cassette.

    Paul et Francine _____ des disques de jazz. Et toi, qu'est-ce que

    tu _____ ?

2. (amener)   Thomas _____ Diane à la boum. Nous _____

    nos cousines. J'_____ Nathalie. Et vous, qui est-ce que

    vous _____ ?

3. (appeler)   Allô! Qui _____-vous? J'_____ Sophie. Éric et André

    _____ leur oncle. Est-ce que tu _____ tes parents?

4. (apercevoir)   Nous _____ nos amis. Moi, j'_____ Pierre.

    Alain _____ Sylvie. Julien et Jean-Michel _____

    leurs amis canadiens. Et vous, qui _____-vous?

Structure

TEST 2 **L'EXAMEN**

There is an important test tomorrow. Say who is preparing for it and who is not. Complete each of the sentences below with the appropriate *affirmative* or *negative* form of the present tense of **se préparer** (*to get ready*).

1. Oui, Jeannette _____ .

2. Oui, ces élèves _____ .

3. Oui, je _____ .

4. Non, vous _____ .

5. Oui, nous _____ .

6. Non, Marc _____ .

7. Oui, tu _____ .

8. Non, ces garçons _____ .

TEST 3 AU CHOIX (*Choose one*)

Read what the following people are doing, and complete the sentences with the *reflexive* or *non-reflexive* pronoun in parentheses that fits logically.

1. Jacques a une voiture. Il _____ lave dans le garage. (se / la)

2. Robert a du savon. Il _____ lave avec ce savon. (se / le)

3. Philippe aime Mathilde. Il _____ regarde souvent. (se / la)

4. Thomas a une glace dans sa chambre. Il _____ regarde souvent dans cette glace. (se / la)

5. M. Arnold a de l'argent. Il _____ met à la banque. (se / le)

6. Catherine a de l'argent. Avec cet argent, elle _____ achète des disques. (s' / l')

7. Le policier voit le bandit. Il _____ arrête. (s' / l')

8. Il n'y a plus d'essence. La voiture _____ arrête. (s' / l')

TEST 4 DEMAIN

Read what the following people are doing today, and say what they are going to do tomorrow. Complete each sentence with the appropriate form of **aller** + *infinitive* of the reflexive verb in italics.

	aujourd'hui:	**demain:**

1. Caroline *se couche* à huit heures.   Elle _____ à dix heures.

2. Mes amis *s'achètent* un magnétophone. Ils _____ des cassettes.

3. Nous *nous levons* tard.   Nous _____ tôt.

4. Je *me prépare* pour l'examen.   Je _____ pour le match de tennis.

TEST 5 À LA BOUM

Éric wants to know if people had fun at his party. Answer him, using the **passé composé** of **s'amuser** in *affirmative* or *negative* sentences. Pay attention to the agreement of the past participle.

1. Robert?   Oui, il _____ .

2. Janine?   Oui, elle _____ .

3. Georges et Vincent? Non, ils _____ .

4. Michèle et Monique? Oui, elles _____ .

5. Toi, Roger?   Oui, je _____ .

6. Toi, Lucie?   Non, je _____ .

TEST 6   EN FRANÇAIS

Write the French equivalent of each of the following sentences, using the appropriate form of the verb in parentheses.

1. *Richard, get ready!*   (se préparer)

   _____

2. *Éric and Marc, do not worry!*   (s'inquiéter)

   _____

3. *We write each other often.*   (s'écrire)

   _____

4. *Pierre and Jacques do not phone each other.*   (se téléphoner)

   _____

5. *Christine is washing her hands.*   (se laver)

   _____

6. *I am brushing my teeth.*   (se brosser)

   _____

Vocabulaire

TEST 7   QU'EST-CE QU'ILS FONT?

Explain what the following people are doing. Complete each sentence with the appropriate form of the *present tense* of the reflexive verb that corresponds to the expression in parentheses.

1. (*is washing*)   Paul _____ .
2. (*is cutting*)   Nathalie _____ les ongles.
3. (*is putting on make-up*)   Annie _____ .
4. (*wakes up*)   Georges _____ à 8 heures.
5. (*is getting up*)   Robert _____ .
6. (*is getting dressed*)   Charlotte _____ pour le concert.
7. (*is shaving*)   Monsieur Renaud _____ .
8. (*is going to bed*)   Nadine _____ .
9. (*is having fun*)   Sylvie _____ avec ses amis.
10. (*is interested*)   René _____ à la musique.
11. (*apologizes*)   Pascal _____ parce qu'il a tort.
12. (*is taking a walk*)   Nicole _____ sur la plage.
13. (*is resting*)   Michèle _____ dans sa chambre.
14. (*remembers*)   Colette _____ de votre cousin.

TEST 8 OÙ?

Complete each sentence below with the name of the *room* or *area* that fits logically.

1. Le réfrigérateur est dans _____ .

2. La voiture est dans _____ .

3. Le sofa est dans _____ .

4. Il y a des jolies roses dans _____ .

5. Je me lave dans _____ .

6. Quand nous avons des invités, nous dînons dans _____ .

TEST 9 ANATOMIE

Complete the following sentences with the names of the appropriate parts of the *body*.

1. Robert a les _____ blonds.

2. Jeannette a les _____ bleus.

3. Richard va chez le dentiste parce qu'il a mal aux _____ .

4. Si vous avez mal à la _____ , prenez de l'aspirine!

5. On écrit avec la _____ .

6. On peut nager sur le _____ ou sur le _____ .

7. Jacques a du chewing-gum dans la _____ .

TESTS DE CONTRÔLE ▪ UNITÉ 4
Verbes

TEST 1   LA BONNE FORME

Complete the sentences below with the appropriate forms of the *present tense* of the verbs in parentheses.

1. (manger)   Nous _____ des fruits. Je _____ une orange.

    Jacques _____ des poires.

2. (envoyer)   J'_____ une lettre à ma sœur. Vous _____ un

    télégramme à vos parents. Mes cousins _____ une carte postale
    à leurs amis.

3. (commencer)   Nous _____ une nouvelle leçon. Vous _____ un

    nouveau livre. La classe _____ à 9 heures.

4. (rire)   Mes amis _____ mais moi, je ne _____ pas.

    Pourquoi _____-vous?

TEST 2   LA PANNE D'ÉLECTRICITÉ (*The power failure*)

There was a power failure yesterday. Say what the following people were doing when it happened. Fill in
each blank with the appropriate *imperfect* form of the verb in parentheses.

1.   (travailler)   Albert et Jean _____ .

2.   (regarder)   Nous _____ la télé.

3.   (écouter)   Vous _____ la radio.

4.   (dîner)   Mes parents _____ .

5.   (finir)   Je _____ une lettre.

6.   (finir)   Nous _____ de dîner.

7.   (attendre)   Vous _____ votre frère.

8.   (répondre)   Jacqueline _____ au téléphone.

9.   (choisir)   Tu _____ un film à la télé.

10. (perdre)   Robert et Alain _____ leur temps.

TEST 3 LE CAMBRIOLAGE

There was a burglary yesterday. A detective wants to know what certain people were doing at the time. Tell him by completing each of the sentences below with the appropriate *imperfect* form of the verb in parentheses.

1. (lire)   Philippe _____ le journal.

2. (écrire) Mme Dupont _____ à sa fille.

3. (dire)   Roland _____ des choses stupides.

4. (prendre) Charles _____ des photos.

5. (boire)   M. Imbert _____ du café.

6. (avoir)   Georges _____ un rendez-vous avec Stéphanie.

7. (faire)   Thomas _____ une promenade.

8. (venir)   Thérèse _____ chez moi.

9. (sortir) Renée _____ avec ses amies.

10. (voir)   Suzanne _____ un film à la télé.

Structure

TEST 4 AVANT

Read what the following people are doing now, and say what they *used to do* before. Fill in each blank with the appropriate *imperfect* form of the verb in italics.

maintenant:	avant:
1. Mes cousins *habitent* à Québec.	Ils _____ à Montréal.
2. M. Renaud *joue* au tennis.	Il _____ au golf.
3. Vous *avez* une voiture de sport.	Vous _____ une moto.
4. Nous *voulons* être architectes.	Nous _____ être professeurs.
5. Je *travaille* dans un restaurant.	Je _____ dans une station-service.
6. Tu *étudies* le français.	Tu _____ l'espagnol.

TEST 5 EN VACANCES

Last summer Henri and his friends spent their vacation on the French Riviera. Say what they did by completing each sentence with **allaient** or **sont allés,** as appropriate.

1. D'habitude, ils _____ à la plage.

2. L'après-midi, ils _____ souvent au café.

3. Un jour, ils _____ à Monaco.

4. Ils _____ à Nice pour le 14 juillet.

5. Le soir, ils _____ généralement au cinéma.

6. Un soir, ils ont rencontré une amie américaine et ils _____ avec elle au restaurant.

TEST 6 HIER

Describe what happened yesterday by filling in each blank with the verb in parentheses that fits logically.

1. Jacques _____ au cinéma avec ses amis. (allait / est allé)

2. Il _____ une heure quand je suis rentré chez moi. (était / a été)

3. Quand vous avez téléphoné, nous _____ . (dînions / avons dîné)

4. Je suis restée chez moi parce qu'il _____ mauvais. (faisait / a fait)

5. Après le dîner, Claire _____ à son petit ami. (téléphonait / a téléphoné)

6. J'ai vu un homme qui _____ un pantalon rouge. (portait / a porté)

TEST 7 RÉSIDENCES

Describe the residences of the following people by completing each sentence with **habite** or **a habité**, as appropriate.

1. Alain _____ à Paris depuis janvier.

2. Robert _____ à Québec depuis 1980.

3. Henri _____ deux ans à Marseille. Après, il est allé à Grenoble.

4. En 1975, mon oncle _____ à New York pendant trois mois.

5. Depuis qu'elle travaille pour Air Canada, Mlle Thierry _____ à Montréal.

TEST 8 EN FRANÇAIS

Complete the French equivalent of each of the following sentences.

1. *My parents visited Cannes fifteen years ago.*

    Mes parents ont visité Cannes _____ .

2. *Marc phoned an hour ago.*

    Marc a téléphoné _____ .

3. *In the past, Pierre often used to go to the movies.*

    Autrefois, Pierre _____ souvent au cinéma.

4. *This week, Annie went twice to the opera.*

    Cette semaine, Annie _____ deux fois à l'opéra.

5. *Georges played tennis and he lost his game.*

    Georges _____ au tennis et il a perdu son match.

6. *Jacques took a picture of his sister when she was playing volleyball.*

    Jacques a pris une photo de sa sœur quand elle _____ au volley.

Vocabulaire

TEST 9   QU'EST-CE QU'ILS FONT?

Describe what the following people are doing. Complete the sentences below with the French equivalent of the verbs in parentheses. Note that these verbs are all in the *present tense* with the exception of items 5 and 6, which are in the **passé composé.**

1. (*sends*)   M. Moreau _____ de l'argent à son fils.

2. (*tries on*)   Marthe _____ un nouveau pull.

3. (*begins*)   Philippe _____ un livre d'aventures.

4. (*chats*)   Nathalie _____ avec Thérèse.

5. (*broke*)   Pierre _____ un vase.

6. (*broke*)   Thomas _____ la jambe.

7. (*jokes*)   Christine _____ avec ses amis.

8. (*cries*)   Mon petit frère _____ .

9. (*smiles*)   Robert _____ parce qu'il vient de parler à sa petite amie.

TEST 10   LA CHAMBRE DE MICHÈLE

Describe the furnishings of Michèle's room by writing out the names of the numbered items. Be sure to use the appropriate definite article.

1. _____
2. _____
3. _____
4. _____
5. _____
6. _____
7. _____
8. _____
9. _____

TEST 11   QUAND?

Complete each of the sentences below with the French equivalent of the expression in parentheses.

1. (*for a long time*)   Nous vous avons attendu _____ .

2. (*once*)   Pierre est allé _____ à Nice.

3. (*twice*)   Roland est allé _____ en Suisse.

4. (*how many times*)   _____ es-tu allée au cinéma cette semaine, Marie?

5. (*in the past*)   _____ , mes parents habitaient en Belgique.

6. (*during*)   J'ai joué au tennis _____ une heure.

7. (*while*)   Sylvie a téléphoné _____ tu étais au cinéma.

8. (*another*)   Nous allons passer _____ semaine à Québec.

TESTS DE CONTRÔLE ▪ UNITÉ 5
Verbes

TEST 1   RÉSIDENCES

Say where the following people live and what they think of their city. Fill in the first blank of each pair of sentences with the appropriate form of **vivre**, and the second blank with the appropriate form of **croire.** Put items 1, 2, and 3 in the *present tense*, and item 4 in the **passé composé.**

1.   Mes cousins _____ à Québec. Ils _____ que c'est une ville très agréable.

2.   Nous _____ à Paris. Nous _____ que c'est une ville splendide.

3.   Tu _____ à Rome. Tu _____ que c'est une très belle ville.

4.   En 1975, Paul _____ à Berlin. Il _____ qu'il allait rester là-bas.

TEST 2   PENDANT LES VACANCES

Say what the following people will do and will not do during vacation. Fill in the first blank of each item with the *affirmative* form of the *future* of the first verb in parentheses. Fill in the second blank with the *negative* form of the *future* of the second verb in parentheses.

1.   (voyager / étudier)   Les élèves _____ . Ils _____ .

2.   (rendre / travailler)   Nous _____ visite à nos grands-parents.

   Nous _____ .

3.   (maigrir / grossir)   Je _____ .

   Je _____ .

4.   (sortir / rester)   Vous _____ souvent.

   Vous _____ à la maison.

5.   (téléphoner / écrire)   Tu _____ à tes cousins.

   Tu _____ à ton professeur.

6.   (apprendre / jouer)   Nicole _____ à faire de la planche à voile.

   Elle _____ au golf.

TEST 3 PROJETS

Several friends are discussing what they *will do* when they are older. Describe their plans by completing each of the sentences below with the appropriate *future* form of the verb in parentheses.

1. (aller)   Gilbert _____ à Tahiti.

2. (être)   Monique _____ architecte.

3. (avoir)   Robert _____ une activité politique.

4. (faire)   Jacqueline _____ du théâtre.

5. (savoir)   Albert _____ faire du ski nautique.

6. (devenir)   Michèle _____ professeur de judo.

7. (voir)   Valérie _____ la Chine et le Japon.

8. (vouloir)   Janine _____ habiter en Suisse.

9. (pouvoir)   Antoine _____ acheter une moto.

10. (devoir)   Suzanne _____ aller à l'université.

TEST 4 RÊVES (*Dreams*)

The following people are dreaming about what they would do if they were to win the lottery. Describe their dreams, using the appropriate *conditional* forms of the verbs in parentheses.

1. (acheter)   Tu _____ une Rolls Royce.

2. (boire)   Mon oncle _____ du champagne.

3. (habiter)   Nous _____ dans une très grande maison.

4. (mettre)   Raoul _____ son argent à la banque.

5. (donner)   Je _____ de l'argent à mes parents.

6. (aider)   Vous _____ vos amis.

7. (avoir)   Marie-Cécile _____ une villa à Saint-Tropez.

8. (aller)   Robert _____ à Hawaii.

Structure

TEST 5 COMPARAISONS

Compare the following people, using the symbols and words in parentheses. Note that these words are *adjectives* in items 1–4, and *nouns* in items 5–8.

1. (+ sympathique)   Jacqueline est _____ son frère.

2. (− riche)   Jeanne est _____ Antoine.

3. (= intelligent)   Robert est _____ son cousin.

4. (+ bon en français) Paul est _____ Thomas.

5. (− argent)   Monique a _____ toi.

6. (+ amis)   J'ai _____ vous.

7. (= disques)   Nous avons _____ René.

8. (+ patience)   Tu as _____ ton frère.

TEST 6   VOYAGES

Read each of the following sentences carefully, and fill in the blank with **Quand** or **Si**, as appropriate.

1. _____ j'ai de l'argent, j'irai aux États-Unis.

2. _____ j'irai aux États-Unis, je passerai à New York.

3. _____ je serai à New York, je visiterai la Statue de la Liberté.

4. _____ je vais en Louisiane, j'irai à la Nouvelle-Orléans.

5. _____ j'irai à la Nouvelle-Orléans, je visiterai le Vieux Carré.

6. _____ je passerai à San Francisco, je rendrai visite à des amis français.

TEST 7   QUESTIONS

Read the following questions and answers very carefully. Then complete each question with **qui** or **quoi,** as appropriate.

questions:	réponses:
1. À _____ penses-tu?	Je pense à l'examen de maths.
2. Avec _____ étudies-tu?	J'étudie avec Marie.
3. De _____ parles-tu?	Je parle de mon cousin.
4. De _____ parles-tu avec lui?	Je parle des vacances.
5. Avec _____ fais-tu ce gâteau?	Je le fais avec des œufs et de la crème.
6. Chez _____ dînes-tu ce soir?	Je dîne chez le voisin.

TEST 8   L'EXPRESSION EXACTE

Read the following questions and answers. Then complete each question with the appropriate interrogative pronoun: **Qui, Qui est-ce que, Qu'est-ce qui,** or **Qu'est-ce que.**

questions:	réponses:
1. _____ est arrivé ce matin?	Une lettre d'Amérique.
2. _____ est allé au restaurant avec toi?	Mon cousin Henri.
3. _____ vous avez mangé?	Du rosbif et de la salade.
4. _____ tu as vu au cinéma?	Un western.
5. _____ a payé les billets?	C'est moi.
6. _____ tu as rencontré là-bas?	Denise et son petit ami.
7. _____ est tombé?	Ton disque.
8. _____ vous avez cassé?	Ce joli vase.

Vocabulaire

TEST 9 LE CONTRAIRE

Complete each of the sentences below with an expression that has the *opposite* meaning of the one in italics.

1. Cet homme est *âgé*. Il n'est pas _____ .

2. Paul est *généreux*. Il n'est pas _____ .

3. Mon cousin est *riche*. Il n'est pas _____ .

4. Jacques est *paresseux*. Il n'est pas _____ .

5. Robert est *faible* en maths. Il n'est pas _____ .

6. Cette voiture est *lente*. Elle n'est pas _____ .

7. Ce disque est *bon marché*. Il n'est pas _____ .

8. Cet exercise est *difficile*. Il n'est pas _____ .

9. Ce vase est *lourd*. Il n'est pas _____ .

10. Christine est *en bonne santé*. Elle n'est pas _____ .

11. Pierre est *nerveux*. Il n'est pas _____ .

12. Richard est *reposé*. Il n'est pas _____ .

13. Alice est *contente*. Elle n'est pas _____ .

TEST 10 MATÉRIAUX

Classify each of the following materials by putting an X in the corresponding column.

	TEXTILES	MÉTAUX PRÉCIEUX	MÉTAUX NON-PRÉCIEUX	AUTRES MATÉRIAUX
⇨ coton	X			
1. aluminium				
2. nylon				
3. argent				
4. bois				
5. verre				
6. fer				
7. laine				
8. pierre				
9. or				
10. cuivre				

TESTS DE CONTRÔLE ▪ UNITÉ 6

Verbes

TEST 1   MAINTENANT ET AVANT

Describe what the following people are doing now and what they did before. Fill in the blanks with the appropriate forms of the verbs in parentheses. Note that the first sentence of each pair is in the *present tense* and the second sentence is in the **passé composé.**

1. (suivre)   Cette année, Thomas _____ un cours d'italien.

     L'année dernière, il _____ un cours d'espagnol.

2. (suivre)   Maintenant, je _____ un régime végétarien.

     Il y a six mois, j'_____ un régime à base de protéines.

3. (ouvrir)   Aujourd'hui, Vincent _____ une lettre.

     Hier, il _____ un télégramme.

4. (souffrir)   Aujourd'hui, vous _____ d'un mal de tête (*headache*).

     Hier soir, vous _____ d'un mal de dents (*toothache*).

Structure

TEST 2   CHRISTINE ET SES AMIS

Say what Christine does for or with her friends. Fill in the blanks with the appropriate *direct* or *indirect* object pronouns that correspond to the people mentioned in parentheses.

1.   (moi)   Christine _____ téléphone souvent.

2.   (nous)   Elle _____ invite chez elle.

3.   (toi)   Elle _____ écrit pour ton anniversaire.

4.   (Paul)   Elle _____ voit assez souvent.

5.   (la sœur de Paul)   Elle _____ parle de ses projets.

6.   (nos cousins)   Elle _____ téléphone.

7.   (Yvette et Monique)   Elle _____ trouve sympathiques.

8.   (ce garçon)   Elle _____ aide.

9.   (ces filles)   Elle _____ montre ses photos.

10. (les amis de Pierre)   Elle _____ critique.

TEST 3 ENTRE AMIS (*Among friends*)

Complete the sentences below by filling in the blanks with the *two object pronouns* that replace the underlined expressions.

1. Je vends <u>mon vélo</u> <u>à Roger</u>.   Je _____ vends.

2. Charles prête <u>ses revues</u> <u>à Nicole</u>.   Il _____ prête.

3. Éric montre <u>sa photo</u> <u>à ses cousins</u>.   Il _____ montre.

4. Claire rend <u>ces livres</u> <u>à ses amies</u>.   Elle _____ rend.

5. Donne <u>ce livre</u> <u>à Jacqueline</u>!   Donne-_____-_____ !

6. Prête <u>tes disques</u> <u>à Paul et à André</u>!   Prête-_____-_____ !

TEST 4 S'IL TE PLAÎT!

Tell a French friend to do, or not to do, the following things for you. Use the appropriate *object pronoun* to replace the words in italics.

▷ prêter *ta raquette*   Oui, _prête-la-moi_ _____ !

1. donner *ton numéro de téléphone*   Oui, _____ !

2. montrer *tes photos*   Oui, _____ !

3. rendre *mon livre* aujourd'hui   Non, _____ aujourd'hui!

4. raconter *cette histoire*   Non, _____ maintenant!

TEST 5 OUI ET NON

Answer the following questions affirmatively or negatively. Use the pronouns **y** or **en** to replace the words in italics.

▷ **Paul est *à Paris*?**   Oui, il _y est_ _____.

1. Nicole est *au restaurant*?   Oui, elle _____.

2. Elle mange *des frites*?   Oui, elle _____.

3. Marc va *à la boulangerie*?   Oui, il _____.

4. Il achète *du pain*?   Oui, il _____.

5. Jacques va *chez ses cousins*?   Non, il _____.

6. Il vient *de la piscine*?   Non, il _____.

7. Robert est allé *au supermarché*?   Oui, il _____.

8. Il a acheté *de la glace*?   Non, il _____.

TEST 6   COMBIEN?

Say how much or how many of the items in italics the people below have. Make complete sentences using the verb **avoir**, the pronoun **en**, and the expression in parentheses.

▷   *des disques?* (2)   Jacques *en a deux* _____ .

1.   *des oranges?* (une douzaine)   Vous _____ .

2.   *du coca?* (une bouteille)   Tu _____ .

3.   *des cassettes?* (beaucoup)   Marc _____ .

4.   *de la limonade?* (un litre)   J'_____ .

5.   *des cousins?* (3)   Nous _____ .

6.   *des voitures?* (1)   Mes parents _____ .

TEST 7   EN FRANÇAIS

Complete the French equivalent of each of the following sentences.

1.   *We work too much!*
     Nous travaillons _____ !

2.   *I don't have much money.*
     Je n'ai pas _____ argent.

3.   *Charles has many jazz records.*
     Charles a _____ disques de jazz.

4.   *You are taking too much champagne!*
     Vous prenez _____ champagne!

5.   *You don't study enough!*
     Tu n'étudies pas _____ !

6.   *Thanks, I have enough meat.*
     Merci, j'ai _____ viande.

7.   *Guillaume likes sports very much.*
     Guillaume _____ .

8.   *Claire often plays tennis.*
     Claire _____ au tennis.

9.   *Marc played well yesterday.*
     Marc _____ hier.

TEST 8   COMMENT?

Complete each of the sentences below with the adverb in **-ment** that corresponds to the adjective in italics.

1.   Maurice est *calme*.   Il parle _____ .

2.   Marc est *rapide*.   Il conduit _____ .

3.   Robert est *normal*.   Il mange _____ .

4.   Georges est *sérieux*.   Il étudie _____ .

5.   Julien est *actif*.   Il travaille _____ .

6.   Mon père est *patient*.   Il m'écoute _____ .

Vocabulaire

TEST 9   QU'EST-CE QU'ILS FONT?

Complete each of the following sentences with the French equivalent of the verb in parentheses.

1.   (*explains*)   Monique _____ la situation à ses amis.

2.   (*dreams*)   Robert _____ d'avoir une moto.

3.   (*hides*)   Albert _____ son argent.

4.   (*closes*)   Nicole _____ la fenêtre.

5.   (*knocks*)   Quelqu'un _____ à la porte.

6.   (*rings*)   Le téléphone _____ .

TEST 10   OÙ?

Complete the sentences below with the names of the appropriate *shopkeepers* (items 1–5) or *stores* (items 6–7).

1.   On achète les fraises et les cerises chez le _____ .

2.   On achète la farine et le riz chez l'_____ .

3.   On achète le pain chez le _____ .

4.   On achète du porc chez le _____ .

5.   On achète le rosbif chez le _____ .

6.   On achète l'aspirine à la _____ .

7.   On achète le parfum et le rouge à lèvres à la _____ .

TESTS DE CONTRÔLE ▪ UNITÉ 7
Verbes

TEST 1   MAINTENANT, AVANT ET APRÈS

Fill in the blanks below with the appropriate forms of the verbs in parentheses. Use the *present tense* in the first sentence of each group, the **passé composé** in the second sentence, and the *future* in the third sentence.

1.   (appartenir)   Maintenant, cette voiture _____ à mon frère.

   Avant, elle _____ à mon père.

   Plus tard, elle _____ à ma sœur.

2.   (obtenir)   Cette semaine, les élèves _____ un «B» à l'examen.

   La semaine dernière, ils _____ un «C».

   La semaine prochaine, ils _____ un «A».

3.   (se tenir)   Aujourd'hui, tu _____ bien en classe.

   Hier, tu _____ assez bien avec tes amis.

   Demain, est-ce que tu _____ bien au concert?

TEST 2   DÉSIRS (*Wishes*)

Describe the wishes of the following people by filling in the blanks with the appropriate *subjunctive* forms of the verbs in parentheses.

1.   (parler / écouter)   Je veux que vous _____ moins et que vous

   _____ mieux.

2.   (finir / réussir)   Le professeur veut que nous _____ les exercices et

   que nous _____ à l'examen.

3.   (téléphoner / répondre)   Je veux que tu me _____ et que

   tu _____ à mes lettres.

4.   (manger / maigrir)   Le docteur Vergne veut que ses malades (*patients*) _____

   moins et qu'ils _____ .

5.   (obéir / aider)   M. Thomas veut que ses enfants _____ et

   qu'ils _____ leur mère.

6.   (vendre / acheter)   Marie veut que son fiancé _____ sa moto et

   qu'il _____ une voiture de sport.

7.   (étudier / choisir)   Mes parents veulent que j'_____ à l'université et

   que je _____ une profession intéressante.

8.   (rendre / inviter)   Mes amis veulent que je leur _____ visite et

   que je les _____ chez moi.

TEST 3 LES DÉSIRS D'ÉRIC

Describe Éric's wishes by completing each of the following sentences with the **il/elle** form of the *subjunctive* of the verb in parentheses.

1. (prendre)   Éric veut que Marc _____ des photos.

2. (sortir)   Il veut que Suzanne _____ avec lui.

3. (partir)   Il veut que son cousin _____ en vacances avec lui.

4. (boire)   Il ne veut pas que Pierre _____ tout le Coca-Cola.

5. (mettre)   Il veut que Thomas _____ un disque de jazz.

6. (venir)   Il veut que Christine _____ chez lui ce soir.

7. (écrire)   Il veut que Nicole lui _____ .

8. (dire)   Il veut que Monique _____ la vérité.

9. (lire)   Il ne veut pas que Claude _____ cette lettre.

10. (voir)   Il veut que Bernadette _____ ce film.

11. (connaître)   Il veut que Lucie _____ ses cousines.

12. (croire)   Il veut que Roland _____ cette histoire.

TEST 4 AVANT LES VACANCES

The following people are leaving for vacation. Tell them what to do, using the appropriate *subjunctive* forms of the verbs in parentheses.

1. (aller)   Il faut que tu _____ en Europe. Il faut que Marc _____ en France. Il faut que nous _____ à Genève. Il faut que Pierre et Annie _____ à Nice.

2. (faire)   Il faut que tu _____ du tennis. Il faut que François _____ des promenades. Il faut que vous _____ du camping. Il faut que Philippe et Jacques _____ de la planche à voile.

3. (être)   Il faut que tu _____ de bonne humeur. Il ne faut pas que Michèle _____ de mauvaise humeur. Il faut que vous _____ prudents. Il faut que Suzanne et Marguerite _____ généreuses avec leurs amis.

4. (avoir)   Il faut que tu _____ un passeport. Il faut que vous _____ vos visas. Il faut que Michel _____ de l'argent. Il faut que Claire et Valérie _____ des traveller-chèques.

Structure

TEST 5 **SENTIMENTS** (*Feelings*)

Describe the feelings that the people below have about their friends. Make complete sentences, using the elements suggested.

1. Marc / être content / nous / organiser une boum.

    _____

2. je / être furieux / vous / partir maintenant

    _____

3. Marie / être heureuse / Philippe / répondre à sa lettre

    _____

4. Antoine / être triste / ses amis / vendre leur voiture

    _____

TEST 6 **MIREILLE**

Everyone has a different opinion of Mireille. Complete each of the sentences below with **est** (*indicative*) or **soit** (*subjunctive*), as appropriate.

1. Jacques sait qu'elle _____ généreuse.

2. Irène pense qu'elle _____ sympathique.

3. Bernard croit qu'elle _____ égoïste.

4. Gilbert a peur qu'elle _____ de mauvaise humeur.

5. Ses parents veulent qu'elle _____ médecin.

6. Je suis heureux qu'elle _____ prudente.

7. Henri est triste qu'elle ne _____ pas son amie.

8. Nous doutons qu'elle _____ d'accord avec nous.

9. Anne ne croit pas qu'elle _____ heureuse.

10. Pensez-vous qu'elle _____ sérieuse?

TEST 7 **TOURISME**

Complete each of the following sentences with **aille** (*subjunctive*) or **aller** (*infinitive*), as appropriate.

1. Je veux _____ au Brésil.

2. Je désire aussi _____ au Pérou.

3. Je veux que Marc _____ là-bas avec nous.

4. Claude veut que j'_____ avec lui en France.

5. Sylviane est heureuse d'_____ en Espagne.

6. Nous ne sommes pas sûrs que Philippe _____ au Portugal.

7. Si vous allez à Paris, il faut _____ à la tour Eiffel.

8. Il faut que Frédéric _____ à Rome.

TEST 8 EN FRANÇAIS

Complete the French equivalent of each of the following sentences.

1. *We are tired of studying.*

   Nous sommes _____ .

2. *Philippe is happy to travel this summer.*

   Philippe est _____ cet été.

3. *It is dangerous to drive too fast!*

   Il est _____ trop vite!

4. *It is impolite to speak all the time.*

   Il est _____ tout le temps!

5. *It is not necessary to be rich in order to be happy.*

   Il n'est pas _____ pour être heureux.

6. *I stayed home because of the test.*

   Je suis resté chez moi _____ l'examen.

7. *Nathalie is working because she wants to earn money.*

   Nathalie travaille _____ elle veut gagner de l'argent.

Vocabulaire

TEST 9 ÉMOTIONS

Describe how the people below feel. Complete each sentence with the French equivalent of the expression in parentheses.

1. (*disappointed*) Jacques est _____ .
2. (*impressed*) Daniel est _____ .
3. (*sorry*) Roger est _____ .
4. (*proud*) Alain est _____ .
5. (*delighted*) Henri est _____ .
6. (*surprised*) Paul est _____ .
7. (*afraid*) Suzanne a _____ .

TEST 10 LA VOITURE

Write out the names of the parts of the car shown below. Use the appropriate article.

1. _____
2. _____
3. _____
4. _____
5. _____
6. _____

TESTS DE CONTRÔLE ▪ UNITÉ 8
Structure

TEST 1   AU GRAND MAGASIN

Imagine that you are in a department store with a French friend. Express your opinion about the various objects in parentheses by completing the sentences with the appropriate form of **celui-ci.**

1.   (une veste)   J'aime beaucoup _____ .

2.   (des chaussures italiennes)   Je n'aime pas _____ .

3.   (des disques français)   J'aimerais écouter _____ .

4.   (un livre)   Je n'ai pas lu _____ .

5.   (une raquette)   Je voudrais jouer avec _____ .

TEST 2   À QUI EST-CE?

Claire is asking Gilbert if certain objects are his. Gilbert tells her that they belong to the people mentioned in parentheses. Complete each of Gilbert's answers with the appropriate form of **celui de.**

	Claire:	**Gilbert:**	
⇨	C'est ton pull?	Non, c'est _celui de Pierre_____ .	**(Pierre)**
1.	C'est ta moto?	Non, c'est _____ .	(Nicole)
2.	Ce sont tes nouveaux disques?	Non, ce sont _____ .	(Antoine)
3.	C'est ton vélo?	Non, c'est _____ .	(mon cousin)
4.	C'est ta guitare?	Non, c'est _____ .	(ma sœur)
5.	Ce sont tes nouvelles lunettes?	Non, ce sont _____ .	(Jacques)

TEST 3   LES PHOTOS DE MARC

Marc is showing his pictures to a friend. Complete his descriptions with **qui** or **que,** as appropriate.

1.   Voici mon cousin _____ habite en Belgique.

2.   Voici l'ami _____ tu as rencontré hier.

3.   Voici des garçons _____ je vois souvent pendant les vacances.

4.   Voici le professeur _____ j'avais l'année dernière.

5.   Voici le vélo _____ j'avais quand j'étais petit.

6.   Voici des maisons _____ sont très anciennes.

TEST 4   PRÉFÉRENCES

Alain asks Olivier if he likes certain things or certain people. Olivier prefers others. Complete Olivier's answers with **celui qui**, **celui que**, **celle qui**, or **celle que**, as appropriate.

Alain: **Olivier:**

1. Tu aimes ce disque?   Je préfère _____ j'ai acheté hier.

2. Tu aimes ce restaurant?   Je préfère _____ est dans l'avenue du Maine.

3. Tu aimes ce professeur?   Je préfère _____ nous avions l'année dernière.

4. Tu aimes cette veste?   Je préfère _____ je porte.

5. Tu aimes cette revue?   Je préfère _____ est sur la table.

6. Tu aimes cette infirmière? Je préfère _____ travaille à l'hôpital Laennec.

TEST 5   QUAND ET COMMENT?

Say when or how people are doing certain things by filling in each blank with the *present participle* of the verb in parentheses.

1. (écouter)   Julien étudie en _____ la radio.

2. (regarder)   Nous dînons en _____ la télé.

3. (attendre)   Vous vous impatientez en _____ vos amis.

4. (vendre)   Béatrice gagne de l'argent en _____ des journaux.

5. (réussir)   Les élèves auront un «A» en _____ à l'examen.

6. (finir)   J'ai trouvé la solution du mystère en _____ le livre.

7. (faire)   Robert maigrit en _____ du sport.

8. (dire)   Tu as raison en _____ la vérité.

9. (conduire)   Faites attention en _____ !

10. (prendre)   J'ai rencontré Paul en _____ l'autobus.

TEST 6   À LA SURPRISE-PARTIE

Complete the following sentences with **danser** or **dansant**, as appropriate.

1. Paul aime _____ .

2. En _____ , Charles parle à Irène.

3. Jacqueline est venue pour _____ .

4. Robert s'amuse en _____ .

5. Philippe est heureux de _____ avec Louise.

6. Avant de _____ , Nicole mange un sandwich.

7. En _____ Robert marche (*steps*) sur les pieds de Thérèse.

8. Marie-Louise se fatigue (*gets tired*) en _____ trop.

TEST 7 EN FRANÇAIS

Complete the French equivalent of each of the following sentences.

1. *I will phone you before going to your house.*

   Je te téléphonerai _____ chez toi.

2. *Jacques is watching TV instead of studying his lessons.*

   Jacques regarde la télé _____ ses leçons.

3. *Nicole is saving money in order to go to Spain this summer.*

   Nicole fait des économies _____ en Espagne cet été.

4. *You will learn Spanish by going to Mexico.*

   Tu apprendras l'espagnol _____ au Mexique.

5. *While going to the movies this afternoon, I saw an accident.*

   _____ au cinéma cet après-midi, j'ai vu un accident.

Vocabulaire

TEST 8 EN VACANCES

Say what the following people are doing during summer vacation. Complete each sentence with the **il/elle** form of the verb that corresponds to the expression in parentheses. Be sure to use **à** or **de,** as appropriate.

1. (*learns how to*) Philippe _____ jouer de la guitare.

2. (*dreams of*) Nicole _____ passer l'été à Tahiti.

3. (*forgets to*) Robert _____ écrire à ses parents.

4. (*begins to*) Monique _____ jouer assez bien au tennis.

5. (*tries to*) Roger _____ maigrir.

6. (*succeeds in*) Gisèle _____ faire de la planche à voile.

7. (*refuses to*) Albert _____ faire du camping avec ses cousins.

8. (*finishes*) Thomas _____ travailler le 18 août.

Complete the sentences with nouns corresponding to the illustrations.

1.

Je n'ai pas besoin de cette _____ parce que j'ai un _____ .

2.

Nicole cherche du _____ pour faire du _____ .

3.

Mes _____ sont dans mon _____ .

4.

Les _____ de cette _____ sont très vieux.

5.

Regarde le _____ et la _____ .

6.

Il y a un _____ dans la _____ .

7.

On ne voit pas le _____ à cause de ce _____ .

8.

La nuit on peut voir la _____ et les _____ .

TESTS DE CONTRÔLE ANSWERS ▪ REPRISE

Answers

TEST 1 Oui et non

1. danse; ne dansent pas
2. travaille; ne travaillez pas
3. maigris; ne maigrissent pas
4. obéissez; n'obéit pas
5. réussissons; ne réussissez pas à l'examen
6. attendent; n'attends pas le professeur
7. répondez; ne réponds pas

TEST 2 S'il vous plaît!

1. Téléphone; Ne réponds pas
2. Travaille; Ne perds pas
3. Maigrissez; Ne grossissez pas
4. Jouez; Ne vendez pas
5. Soyez; Ne soyez pas

TEST 3 Catherine et ses amis

1. est; a; va
2. sont; ont; vont
3. sommes; avons; allons
4. êtes; avez; allez

TEST 4 Questions et réponses

1. Où est-ce que tu habites
2. Est-ce que vous parlez français
3. Comment est-ce que Jacques voyage
4. Qu'est-ce que tes amis écoutent
5. À qui est-ce que tu téléphones
6. Est-ce que Charles habite à Québec

TEST 5 Qu'est-ce qu'ils ont?

1. des cousines <u>intéressantes</u>
2. une <u>petite</u> voiture
3. des <u>jolies</u> robes
4. des amies <u>anglaises</u>
5. des disques <u>français</u>

TEST 6 Qu'est-ce qu'ils font?

1. parle <u>aux</u> élèves
2. allons <u>à la</u> piscine
3. jouez <u>au</u> tennis
4. rentrons <u>de la</u> plage
5. joue <u>du</u> piano
6. parlons <u>aux</u> frères <u>des</u> garçons français

TEST 7 Descriptions

1. C'est; Elle est
2. Il est; C'est
3. Elle est; C'est
4. C'est; Il est

TEST 8 Qui?

1. elle
2. lui
3. elle; lui
4. il; eux
5. Il; elles
6. Elle; lui

TEST 9 En famille

1. nos; notre
2. sa; son
3. son; son
4. leurs
5. votre; vos

Interpretation

If you made any mistakes in the forms of:
-er verbs: review Structure A, page 6;
-ir verbs: review Structure B, page 47;
-re verbs: review Structure C, page 48.
If you made any mistakes in the negative forms, review Structure A, page 6.

If you made any mistakes in:
Items 1–4: review Structure D, page 12;
Item 5: review the imperative of **être** in Structure A, page 18.

If you made any mistakes in the forms of **être** or **avoir**, review Structure A, page 18.
If you made any mistakes in the forms of **aller**, review Structure B, page 30.

If you made any mistakes in the word order, review Structure C, page 10.
If you made any mistakes in the question words, review the Vocabulaire on page 10.

If you made any mistakes in the form or the position of the underlined adjectives, review Structure C, page 22.

If you made any mistakes in the underlined words, review Structure A, page 29.

If you made any mistakes, review Structure D, page 24.

If you made any mistakes, review Structure A, page 37.

If you made any mistakes, review Structure D, page 40.

TEST 10   Géographie

1. au Canada
2. les États-Unis
3. d'Allemagne
4. le Mexique
5. aux États-Unis
6. en Espagne

If you made any mistakes, review Structure C and the Vocabulaire on page 32.

TEST 11   En français

1. n'ai pas de cassettes
2. n'a pas d'amis
3. les sports; le tennis
4. chez moi
5. chez Éric
6. va jouer; n'allons pas jouer
7. les disques de Pierre
8. la sœur de Marie

If you made any mistakes in:
Items 1–3: review Structure B, page 19;
Items 4–5: review Structure B, page 38;
Item 6: review Structure B, page 30;
Items 7–8: review Structure C, page 38.

TEST 12   Activités

1. regarde
2. écoute
3. téléphone à
4. travaille
5. obéit à
6. attend
7. rend visite à
8. répond à

If you made any mistakes (including the use of à) in:
Items 1–4: review the Vocabulaire on pages 4–5;
Item 5: review the Vocabulaire on page 47;
Items 6–8: review the Vocabulaire on page 48.

TEST 13   Leurs possessions

1. un vélo (une bicyclette); un appareil-photo
2. un chien; un chat
3. un anorak; des bottes
4. des lunettes de soleil; un maillot de bain
5. un chapeau; une cravate

If you made any mistakes in:
Items 1–2: review the Vocabulaire on pages 20–21;
Items 3–5: review the Vocabulaire on pages 44–45.

TEST 14   Avant et après

1. neuf; onze
2. quinze; dix-sept
3. dix-neuf; vingt et un
4. soixante-dix-neuf; quatre-vingt-un
5. dimanche; mardi
6. mercredi; vendredi
7. janvier; mars
8. juin; août
9. été; hiver
10. le premier décembre; le trois décembre

If you made any mistakes in:
Item 1: review the vocabulary on page 13;
Items 2–3: review the vocabulary on page 25;
Item 4: review the vocabulary on page 50;
Items 5–6: review the vocabulary on page 33;
Items 7–10: review the vocabulary on page 41.

TESTS DE CONTRÔLE ANSWERS ▪ UNITÉ 1

Answers

Interpretation

TEST 1   Week-end

1. veut; veulent; voulons; veux
2. devons; dois; doivent; devez
3. peuvent; peux; pouvons; pouvez

If you made any mistakes, review Structure C, page 70.

TEST 2   Qu'est-ce qu'ils font?

1. faisons; fait; font; faites
2. viennent; vient; venez
3. sortons; sors; sortent; sors
4. prenons; prend; prennent; prends
5. conduisent; conduit; conduisez
6. mets; mettent; mettez
7. buvons; bois; boivent; buvez

If you made any mistakes in:
Item 1: review Structure D, page 63;
Item 2: review Structure B, page 91;
Item 3: review Structure A, page 90;
Item 4: review Structure A, page 60;
Item 5: review Structure A, page 68;
Item 6: review Structure A, page 85;
Item 7: review Structure C, page 62.

TEST 3   Hier

1. avons étudié; n'avons pas regardé
2. a travaillé; n'a pas perdu
3. ont acheté; n'ont pas choisi
4. avez écouté; n'avez pas fini
5. as rendu; n'as pas attendu
6. ai vendu; n'ai pas acheté
7. a choisi; n'a pas dépensé
8. ont joué; n'ont pas gagné

If you made 2 or more mistakes, review Structure B, page 78.

TEST 4 L'été dernier

1. a fait
2. a été
3. a eu
4. a appris
5. a conduit
6. a bu
7. a mis
8. a voulu
9. a dû
10. a pu

If you made 2 or more mistakes, review Structure B, page 86.

TEST 5 Où sont-ils allés?

1. est allée; est sortie
2. est allé; a acheté
3. sont allés; sont rentrés
4. sont allées; sont restées
5. sommes allés; avons nagé
6. êtes allés; êtes venus

If you made any mistakes in the passé composé of **aller,** review Structure C, pages 92–93.

If you made any mistakes in the passé composé of the other verbs, review the Vocabulaire on page 93.

TEST 6 Au restaurant

1. du rosbif
2. de caviar
3. des spaghetti
4. d'œufs
5. de la salade
6. de glace

If you made any mistakes, review Structure B, page 61.

TEST 7 Article partitif ou article défini?

1. la
2. du
3. des
4. Le
5. du
6. de l'
7. de l'
8. La

If you made any mistakes, review Structure B, page 61.

TEST 8 En français

1. on parle
2. on est; on aime
3. est architecte
4. être professeur
5. il faut (on doit)
6. il faut (vous devez, on doit)
7. a froid
8. ai raison
9. Est-ce qu'Hélène a parlé
10. Est-ce qu'ils ont joué (Ont-ils joué)
11. Je viens de parler
12. viennent d'acheter

If you made any mistakes in:
Items 1–2: review Structure B, page 69;
Items 3–4: review the Notes de Vocabulaire on page 72;
Items 5–6: review Structure D, page 71;
Items 7–8: review the Vocabulaire on page 77;
Items 9–10: review Structure C, page 80;
Items 11–12: review Structure B, page 91.

TEST 9 L'intrus

1. boit
2. mange
3. traduit
4. prend
5. dure
6. permet
7. met
8. tombe

If you made any mistakes, review the verbs in the unit, both in the Structure sections and in the Vocabulaires.

TEST 10 Les amis de Simone

1. fait les courses
2. fait un voyage
3. fait une promenade
4. faire la cuisine
5. a sommeil
6. a soif
7. a chaud
8. a envie de

If you made any mistakes in:
Items 1–4: review Section D, pages 63–64;
Items 5–8: review the Vocabulaire on page 77.

TEST 11 Catégories

1. le jambon, le poulet, le rosbif
2. le thon, la sole
3. les petits pois, les haricots, les carottes, les pommes de terre, les tomates, le céleri
4. une banane, une orange, une poire, une pomme
5. le beurre, le fromage, le yaourt, la glace, le lait
6. le petit déjeuner, le déjeuner, le dîner
7. le Coca-Cola, la limonade, le jus d'orange, le café, le lait, le thé, l'eau, l'eau minérale, le jus de fruits
8. le vin, la bière
9. le ski nautique, la natation, la planche à voile, la voile
10. le ski, le patin à glace

If you made any mistakes in:
Items 1–6: review the Vocabulaires on pages 58–59 and 63;
Items 7–8: review the Vocabulaire on page 63;
Items 9–10: review the Vocabulaire on page 64.

TESTS DE CONTRÔLE ANSWERS ■ UNITÉ 2

Answers

TEST 1   Qu'est-ce qu'ils font?

1. lis; lisent; lis
2. écrivons; écris; écrivent
3. dites; dis; disent
4. voit; voient; voyez
5. connaissent; connaissez; connaît
6. sais; savez; savent

TEST 2   Hier

1. a lu   4. a vu
2. a écrit   5. a reconnu
3. a dit   6. a su

TEST 3   Jacqueline

1. nouvelle; nouvel; nouveaux; nouvelles
2. vieilles; vieil; vieille
3. belle; belles; beau; beaux

TEST 4   Ressemblance

1. originaux   5. sportive
2. loyales   6. musiciennes
3. curieuse   7. ponctuelle
4. généreux   8. mignonne

TEST 5   Entre amis

1. l'invite   7. l'aider
2. les connaît   8. les voir
3. ne le connais pas   9. l'a vue
4. la trouvons   10. ne l'a pas aidé
5. Invite-la   11. les as rencontrés
6. Ne les invitons pas   12. ne les avez pas vues

TEST 6   Les amis de Marc

1. lui   3. les   5. leur   7. le
2. lui   4. l'   6. leur   8. lui

TEST 7   Qui ou que?

1. que   3. qui   5. que   7. qui
2. qui   4. que   6. qui

TEST 8   En français

1. connais; ne sais pas   5. n'habite plus
2. sais   6. ne fait rien
3. n'étudie jamais   7. ne parle à personne
4. n'a jamais visité

TEST 9   Jacques et ses amis

1. trouve   6. demande
2. rencontre   7. prête
3. oublie   8. présente
4. cherche   9. donne
5. aide   10. montre

Interpretation

If you made any mistakes in:
Items 1–3: review Structure A, page 115;
Item 4: review Structure A, page 122;
Item 5: review Structure B, page 123;
Item 6: review Structure A, page 130.

If you made any mistakes in:
Items 1–3: review Structure A, page 115;
Item 4: review Structure A, page 122;
Item 5: review Structure B, page 123;
Item 6: review Structure A, page 130.

If you made 2 or more mistakes, review Structure A, page 136.

If you made 2 or more mistakes, review Structure A, page 142.

If you made any mistakes in the *form* of the pronouns, review Structure C, page 124.
If you made any mistakes in the *position* of the pronouns in Items 1–8, review the notes in Structure C, page 124.
If you made any mistakes in the *position* of the pronouns and the agreement of the past participle in Items 9–12, review Structure D, page 126.

If you made any mistakes, review Structure C, page 124, Structure B, page 131, and the Vocabulaires on pages 125 and 132.

If you made any mistakes in:
Items 1, 4, 5: review Structure C, page 138;
Items 2, 3, 6, 7: review Structure B, page 137.

If you made any mistakes in:
Items 1–2: review Structure A, page 130;
Items 3–5: review Structure B, page 143;
Items 6–7: review the Vocabulaire on page 144.

If you made any mistakes in:
Items 1–5: review the Vocabulaire on page 125;
Items 6–10: review the Vocabulaire on page 132.

TESTS DE CONTRÔLE ANSWERS • UNITÉ 3

Answers

TEST 1   Aujourd'hui

1. achetons; achète; achètent; achètes
2. amène; amenons; amène; amenez
3. appelez; appelle; appellent; appelles
4. apercevons; aperçois; aperçoit; aperçoivent; apercevez

TEST 2   L'examen

1. se prépare
2. se préparent
3. me prépare
4. ne vous préparez pas
5. nous préparons
6. ne se prépare pas
7. te prépares
8. ne se préparent pas

TEST 3   Au choix

1. la   3. la   5. le   7. l'
2. se   4. se   6. s'   8. s'

TEST 4   Demain

1. va <u>se coucher</u>
2. vont <u>s'acheter</u>
3. allons <u>nous lever</u>
4. vais <u>me préparer</u>

TEST 5   À la boum

1. s'est amusé
2. s'est amusée
3. ne se sont pas amusés
4. se sont amusées
5. me suis amusé
6. ne me suis pas amusée

TEST 6   En français

1. Richard, prépare-toi!
2. Éric et Marc, ne vous inquiétez pas!
3. Nous nous écrivons souvent.
4. Pierre et Jacques ne se téléphonent pas.
5. Christine se lave les mains.
6. Je me brosse les dents.

TEST 7   Qu'est-ce qu'ils font?

1. se lave
2. se coupe
3. se maquille
4. se réveille
5. se lève
6. s'habille
7. se rase
8. se couche
9. s'amuse
10. s'intéresse
11. s'excuse
12. se promène
13. se repose
14. se souvient

TEST 8   Où?

1. la cuisine
2. le garage
3. le salon (la salle de séjour)
4. le jardin
5. la salle de bains
6. la salle à manger

TEST 9   Anatomie

1. cheveux   3. dents   5. main   7. bouche
2. yeux   4. tête   6. ventre; dos

Interpretation

If you made any mistakes in:
Items 1–2: review Structure A, page 155;
Item 3: review Structure B, page 164;
Item 4: review Structure A, page 174.

If you made any mistakes, review Structure C, page 157.

If you made any mistakes, review Structure B, pages 156–157.

If you made any mistakes in the form of the infinitive, review Structure D, page 177.

If you made any mistakes, review Structure B, page 182.

If you made any mistakes in:
Items 1–2: review Structure A, page 163;
Items 3–4: review Structure A, page 180;
Items 5–6: review Structure B, page 170.

If you made any mistakes in:
Items 1–2: review the Vocabulaire on page 153;
Items 3–8: review the Vocabulaire on page 168;
Items 9–10: review the Vocabulaire on page 175;
Items 11–14: review the Vocabulaire on page 176.

If you made any mistakes, review the Vocabulaire on page 154.

If you made any mistakes, review the Vocabulaire on page 170.

TESTS DE CONTRÔLE ANSWERS ▪ UNITÉ 4

Answers

TEST 1   La bonne forme

1. mangeons; mange; mange
2. envoie; envoyez; envoient
3. commençons; commencez; commence
4. rient; ris; riez

TEST 2   La panne d'électricité

1. travaillaient
2. regardions
3. écoutiez
4. dînaient
5. finissais
6. finissions
7. attendiez
8. répondait
9. choisissais
10. perdaient

TEST 3   Le cambriolage

1. lisait
2. écrivait
3. disait
4. prenait
5. buvait
6. avait
7. faisait
8. venait
9. sortait
10. voyait

TEST 4   Avant

1. habitaient
2. jouait
3. aviez
4. voulions
5. travaillais
6. étudiais

TEST 5   En vacances

1. allaient
2. allaient
3. sont allés
4. sont allés
5. allaient
6. sont allés

TEST 6   Hier

1. est allé
2. était
3. dînions
4. faisait
5. a téléphoné
6. portait

TEST 7   Résidences

1. habite
2. habite
3. a habité
4. a habité
5. habite

TEST 8   En français

1. il y a quinze ans
2. il y a une heure
3. allait
4. est allé
5. a joué
6. jouait

TEST 9   Qu'est-ce qu'ils font?

1. envoie
2. essaie
3. commence
4. bavarde
5. a cassé
6. s'est cassé
7. plaisante
8. pleure
9. sourit

TEST 10   La chambre de Michèle

1. le lit
2. la chaise
3. la commode
4. la bibliothèque
5. la lampe
6. la machine à écrire
7. le tapis
8. le poster (l'affiche)
9. les rideaux

TEST 11   Quand?

1. longtemps
2. une fois
3. deux fois
4. Combien de fois
5. Autrefois
6. pendant
7. pendant que
8. une autre

Interpretation

If you made any mistakes in:
Items 1–3: review Structure A, page 203;
Item 4: review Structure A, page 226.

If you made any mistakes, review Structure A, page 208.

If you made any mistakes, review Structure A, pages 208–209. If you have forgotten the **nous** form of the present tense of these verbs, review them in Appendix 4.C, pages 420–427.

If you made any mistakes, review Structure A, page 215.

If you made any mistakes, review Structure A, page 215.

If you made any mistakes, review Structure B, page 216, and Structure A, page 220.

If you made any mistakes, review Structure B, page 227.

If you made any mistakes in:
Items 1–2: review Structure B, page 204;
Items 3–6: review Structure B, page 222.

If you made any mistakes in:
Items 1–3: review the Vocabulaire on page 203;
Items 4–6: review the Vocabulaire on page 213;
Items 7–9: review the Vocabulaire on page 226.

If you made 2 or more mistakes, review the Vocabulaire on page 214.

If you made any mistakes in:
Items 1–5: review the Vocabulaire on page 205;
Items 6–8: review the Vocabulaire on page 219.

Answers

Interpretation

TEST 1 Résidences

1. vivent; croient
2. vivons; croyons
3. vis; crois
4. a vécu; a cru

If you made any mistakes in the forms of **vivre**, review Structure B, page 257.
If you made any mistakes in the forms of **croire**, review Structure A, page 264.

TEST 2 Pendant les vacances

1. voyageront; n'étudieront pas
2. rendrons; ne travaillerons pas
3. maigrirai; ne grossirai pas
4. sortirez; ne resterez pas
5. téléphoneras; n'écriras pas
6. apprendra; ne jouera pas

If you made any mistakes, review Structure A, pages 244–245, and Structure B, page 246.

TEST 3 Projets

1. ira	4. fera	7. verra	10. devra
2. sera	5. saura	8. voudra	
3. aura	6. deviendra	9. pourra	

If you made any mistakes in:
Items 1–4: review Structure A, page 250;
Items 5–10: review Structure A, page 256.

TEST 4 Rêves

1. achèterais	4. mettrait	7. aurait
2. boirait	5. donnerais	8. irait
3. habiterions	6. aideriez	

If you made any mistakes, review Structure C, page 266.

TEST 5 Comparaisons

1. plus sympathique que	5. moins d'argent que
2. moins riche qu'	6. plus d'amis que
3. aussi intelligent que	7. autant de disques que
4. meilleur en français que	8. plus de patience que

If you made any mistakes in:
Items 1–4: review Structure A, page 236;
Items 5–8: review Structure B, page 238.

TEST 6 Voyages

1. Si	3. Quand	5. Quand
2. Quand	4. Si	6. Quand

If you made any mistakes, review Structure B, page 251, and Structure C, page 252.

TEST 7 Questions

1. quoi	3. qui	5. quoi
2. qui	4. quoi	6. qui

If you made any mistakes, review Structure C, page 259.

TEST 8 L'expression exacte

1. Qu'est-ce qui	5. Qui
2. Qui	6. Qui est-ce que
3. Qu'est-ce que	7. Qu'est-ce qui
4. Qu'est-ce que	8. Qu'est-ce que

If you made 2 or more mistakes, review Structures D and E, page 260.

TEST 9 Le contraire

1. jeune	6. rapide	10. malade
2. égoïste	7. cher	11. calme
3. pauvre	8. facile	12. fatigué
4. travailleur	9. léger	13. triste (malheureuse)
5. fort		

If you made 2 or more mistakes in Items 1–9, review the Vocabulaire on pages 236–237.
If you made any mistakes in Items 10–13, review the Vocabulaire on page 249.

TEST 10 Matériaux

TEXTILES: nylon, laine
MÉTAUX PRÉCIEUX: argent, or
MÉTAUX NON-PRÉCIEUX: aluminium, fer, cuivre
AUTRES MATÉRIAUX: bois, verre, pierre

If you made any mistakes, review the Vocabulaire on page 258.

TESTS DE CONTRÔLE ANSWERS ▪ UNITÉ 6

TEST 1   Maintenant et avant

1. suit; a suivi   3. ouvre; a ouvert
2. suis; ai suivi   4. souffrez; avez souffert

If you made any mistakes in:
Items 1–2: review Structure A, page 288;
Items 3–4: review Structure A, page 296.

TEST 2   Christine et ses amis

1. me	4. le	7. les	10. les
2. nous	5. lui	8. l'	
3. t'	6. leur	9. leur	

If you made 2 or more mistakes, review Structure B,
pages 289–290.

TEST 3   Entre amis

1. le lui	3. la leur	5. le-lui
2. les lui	4. les leur	6. les-leur

If you made any mistakes, review Structure B,
pages 296–297.

TEST 4   S'il te plaît!

1. donne-le-moi   3. ne me le rends pas
2. montre-les-moi   4. ne me la raconte pas

If you made any mistakes, review Structure D,
page 299.

TEST 5   Oui et non

1. *y* est	4. *en* achète	7. *y* est allé
2. *en* mange	5. n'*y* va pas	8. n'*en* a pas
3. *y* va	6. n'*en* vient pas	

If you made any mistakes in:
Items 1, 3, 5, 7: review Structure A, page 302;
Items 2, 4, 6, 8: review Structure C, page 306.

TEST 6   Combien?

1. *en avez une douzaine*	4. *en ai un litre*
2. *en as une bouteille*	5. *en avons trois*
3. *en a beaucoup*	6. *en ont une*

If you made any mistakes in:
Items 1–4: review Structure B, page 311;
Items 5–6: review Structure C, page 312.

TEST 7   En français

1. trop	5. assez	8. joue souvent
2. beaucoup d'	6. assez de	9. a bien joué
3. beaucoup de	7. aime beaucoup	
4. trop de	les sports	

If you made any mistakes in:
Items 1–6: review Structure A, page 310;
Items 7–9 (position of adverbs): review Structure C,
pages 318–319.

TEST 8   Comment?

1. calmement	3. normalement	5. activement
2. rapidement	4. sérieusement	6. patiement

If you made any mistakes, review Structure B,
page 317.

TEST 9   Qu'est-ce qu'ils font?

1. explique	3. cache	5. frappe
2. rêve	4. ferme	6. sonne

If you made any mistakes in:
Items 1–2: review the Vocabulaire on page 286;
Items 3–6: review the Vocabulaire on page 294.

TEST 10   Où?

1. marchand de fruits	4. charcutier	7. parfumerie
2. épicier	5. boucher	
3. boulanger	6. pharmacie	

If you made 2 or more mistakes, review the
Vocabulaire on pages 304–305.

TESTS DE CONTRÔLE ANSWERS ▪ UNITÉ 7

TEST 1   Maintenant, avant et après

1. appartient; a appartenu; appartiendra
2. obtiennent; ont obtenu; obtiendront
3. te tiens; t'es tenu; te tiendra

If you made any mistakes, review Structure A,
page 328.

TEST 2 Désirs

1. parliez; écoutiez
2. finissions; réussissions
3. téléphones; répondes
4. mangent; maigrissent
5. obéissent; aident
6. vende; achète
7. étudie; choisisse
8. rende; invite

If you made any mistakes, review Structure A, pages 334–335.

TEST 3 Les désirs d'Éric

1. prenne
2. sorte
3. parte
4. boive
5. mette
6. vienne
7. écrive
8. dise
9. lise
10. voie
11. connaisse
12. croie

If you made any mistakes, review Structure A, pages 334–335.
You may also want to review the **ils** form of the present tense of these verbs in Appendix 4.C on pages 420–427.

TEST 4 Avant les vacances

1. ailles; aille; allions; aillent
2. fasses; fasse; fassiez; fassent
3. sois; soit; soyez; soient
4. aies; ayez; ait; aient

If you made any mistakes in:
Items 1–2: review Structure A, page 351;
Items 3–4: review Structure B, page 343.

TEST 5 Sentiments

1. Marc est content que nous organisions une boum.
2. Je suis furieux que vous partiez maintenant.
3. Marie est heureuse que Philippe réponde à sa lettre.
4. Antoine est triste que ses amis vendent leur voiture.

If you made any mistakes in the underlined expressions, review Structure A, page 342, and Structure B, page 352.

TEST 6 Mireille

1. est
2. est
3. est
4. soit
5. soit
6. soit
7. soit
8. soit
9. soit
10. soit

If you made 2 or more mistakes, review Structure B, page 359. If necessary, go back to the appropriate sections of the unit.

TEST 7 Tourisme

1. aller
2. aller
3. aille
4. aille
5. aller
6. aille
7. aller
8. aille

If you made any mistakes, review Structure B, page 359. If necessary, go back to the appropriate sections of the unit.

TEST 8 En français

1. fatigués d'étudier
2. content (heureux) de voyager
3. dangereux de conduire
4. impoli de parler
5. nécessaire d'être riche
6. à cause de
7. parce qu'

If you made any mistakes in:
Items 1–2: review Structure B, page 329;
Items 3–5: review Structure C, page 330;
Items 6–7: review the Note de Vocabulaire on page 356.

TEST 9 Émotions

1. déçu
2. impressionné
3. désolé
4. fier
5. ravi
6. surpris (étonné)
7. peur

If you made any mistakes in:
Items 1–2: review the Vocabulaire on page 333;
Items 3–7: review the Vocabulaire on page 352.

TEST 10 La voiture

1. le moteur
2. le phare
3. le siège
4. la roue
5. le coffre
6. le pneu

If you made 2 or more mistakes, review the Vocabulaire on page 350.

TESTS DE CONTRÔLE ANSWERS ▪ UNITÉ 8

Answers

Interpretation

TEST 1 Au grand magasin

1. celle-ci
2. celles-ci
3. ceux-ci
4. celui-ci
5. celle-ci

If you made any mistakes, review Structure B, page 380.

TEST 2   À qui est-ce?

1. celle de Nicole   4. celle de ma sœur
2. ceux d'Antoine   5. celles de Jacques
3. celui de mon cousin

If you made any mistakes, review Structure C, pages 380–381.

TEST 3   Les photos de Marc

1. qui   3. que   5. que
2. que   4. que   6. qui

If you made any mistakes, review Structure A, page 385.

TEST 4   Préférences

1. celui que   3. celui que   5. celle qui
2. celui qui   4. celle que   6. celle qui

If you made any mistakes, review Structure B, page 386.

TEST 5   Quand et comment?

1. écoutant   5. réussissant   8. disant
2. regardant   6. finissant   9. conduisant
3. attendant   7. faisant   10. prenant
4. vendant

If you made any mistakes, review Structure A, page 402. You may also want to review the **nous** form of the present tense of the verbs in items 7–10 in Appendix 4.C, pages 420–427.

TEST 6   À la surprise-partie

1. danser   3. danser   5. danser   7. dansant
2. dansant   4. dansant   6. danser   8. dansant

If you made any mistakes, review Structure B, page 403.

TEST 7   En français

1. avant d'aller   4. en allant
2. au lieu d'étudier 5. En allant
3. pour aller

If you made any mistakes in:
Items 1–3: review Structure A, pages 397–398;
Items 4–5: review Structure B, page 403.

TEST 8   En vacances

1. apprend à   4. commence à   7. refuse de
2. rêve de   5. essaie de   8. finit de (cesse de)
3. oublie d'   6. réussit à

If you made 2 or more mistakes, review Structure B, page 391, and the Vocabulaire on page 392.

TEST 9   Dehors

1. couverture;   5. canard; rivière
   sac de couchage 6. cheval; prairie
2. bois; feu   7. soleil; nuage
3. jumelles; sac à dos   8. lune; étoiles
4. arbres; forêt

If you made any mistakes in:
Items 1–3: review the Vocabulaire on page 378;
Items 4–6: review the Vocabulaire on page 389;
Items 7–8: review the Vocabulaire on pages 396–397.